PRODUCING
THE PROMISE

PRODUCING THE PROMISE

Liberty Savard

Bridge-Logos *Publishers*

North Brunswick, New Jersey 08902 USA

Producing the Promise

by Liberty Savard
International Standard Book Number: 0-88270-780-9
Library of Congress Catalog Card Number: 99-64055
Copyright ©1999 by Liberty Savard

Published by:
Bridge-Logos *Publishers*
North Brunswick Corporate Center
1300 Airport Road, Suite E
North Brunswick, NJ 08902-1700
http://www.bridgelogos.com

Dedication

I dedicate this book to my faithful armor bearer, Evelyn Christian. She has been dedicated, willing to pray, loyal, and always teachable during travels across the nation, the writing of my books, transition periods, putting out newsletters, and painful spiritual growth. I have always been able to count on her and I am grateful.

The Keys of the Kingdom Trilogy
by Liberty Savard:

• *Shattering Your Strongholds*

• *Breaking the Power*

• *Producing the Promise*

Also available:

• *Shattering Your Strongholds Workbook*

Coming soon:

• *Breaking the Power Workbook*

For further information on speaking engagements, seminars, current U.S. itinerary, teaching tapes, workbooks, television programs, and free teaching newsletters published quarterly, please contact:

Liberty Savard Ministries, Inc.
(a non-profit organization)
P.O. Box 41260
Sacramento, CA 95841-0260

Office phone: 916-721-7770
Facsimile: 916-721-8889

E-mail: liberty@libertysavard.com
Web site: http://www.libertysavard.com

Table of Contents

Introduction

It has been exciting to hear from people whose lives and families have been dramatically changed by the first two books of the keys of the Kingdom trilogy, *Shattering Your Strongholds* (Bridge-Logos Publishers, 1993) and *Breaking the Power* (Bridge-Logos Publishers, 1997). Some readers contact our ministry office, however, with great indignation over my even thinking of reconstructing some of the church world's most revered humanistic doctrines. That can be sobering, yet it always gives me a desire to pray that God's will would be done in their lives; not my will, not their will, but God's will. Most who take the time to respond are thrilled. After years of seeking for answers to unmet needs, unanswered prayers, unresolved issues, and unhealed hurts, they see that here is something to finally help them break free of their old stuff. They are excited that the keys of the Kingdom are within their reach, and they have the courage to take them up and use them! This is always rewarding and refreshing.

The following letter provided great encouragement: "I am a pastor, and while I don't have time to tell you my life story, suffice it to say that God has had to let me go through hard, hard times—thanks to my own unsurrendered soul. I've been a people pleaser most of my life, and you want to talk about soul-ties and wrong relationships! I and my bride of 29 years have been so hurt, wounded, rejected, and betrayed since we have been in the ministry. All my life, I have begged God to teach me to pray. My prayers were mostly flares that I shot up to God hoping He would see them and do something to help me. <u>Then</u> someone shared your books with me—God had graciously answered my prayer. The light immediately went on for me as I devoured both books twice. I was so excited that I began binding and loosing everything in sight!

"I shared your concepts with my church family and begged them to start praying this way. The results have been incredible. We have seen marriages restored, people saved, mean bosses turned into pussycats, finances come forth . . . and on and on. Every day someone calls to share another answer to prayer. <u>Faith is skyrocketing here because we are finally praying</u> EFFECTUALLY! Praise Him! Please come to North Carolina and teach us more."

Nothing I could say about the powerful results of praying these principles could be any more heartfelt than this pastor's letter, adding to the thousands of answers to prayers that have poured into our ministry since the first book of this trilogy was released in January of 1993. The office staff has seen reports of miracle breakthroughs come in by mail, phone, e-mail, with some even coming in person. One such man who had attended meetings in Ohio came to San Francisco this spring. He determined before he left Ohio that he was going to drive to Sacramento to get more books and tell us how the principles were changing his life. What a treat for us!

Relationship and Receiving

The intent of my writings is to show believers how simple Jesus Christ has always wanted our Christian walk to be. *Shattering Your Strongholds* focused on learning the power of the keys of the Kingdom when applied to getting our own souls free from the half truths and wrong patterns of thinking we've learned from our families, the church world, and the conventional wisdom of the world around us. *Breaking the Power* attempted to challenge our misunderstandings of some of the wrong road maps we've been following in the church world for years, laying out a clear definition of the path between the soul and the spirit of man.

Both books stressed the truth of the deeper purposes of the keys of binding and loosing as revealed to us in Matthew 16:19 and 18:18. This truth has resulted in dysfunctional families learning how to come together, many getting on track with their destiny purposes, and individuals recognizing that blaming the devil has been an escape mechanism used by our unsurrendered souls to avoid accountability for perpetuating our pain and our bondage. We have allowed our souls to make our Christianity complicated and self-centered, believing our Christian victory to be hindered at every turn by evil spirits, believing ourselves to be weak or strong according to our personal failures or successes.

Christianity is not about legalistic rules and regulations, nor is it about sloppy agape and grace to keep making wrong choices. Christianity is about relationshp and receiving. And the unsurrendered soul simply does not want to give up any of its control over unresolved, unrevenged traumatic memories to allow room to be created to receive a new King upon the throne of our lives. Leaving the depth of our spiritual relationship with God up to our souls is like leaving a wolf in charge of feeding the chickens!

In Paul's epistle to the Galatian Christians, *The Message* translates Galatians chapter 3:11-12 like this, *"The obvious impossibility of carrying out such a moral program* (the rules and regulations of the Old Testament Law) *should make it plain that no one can sustain a relationship with God that way. The person who lives in right relationship with God does it by embracing what God arranges for him. Doing things for God is the opposite of entering into what God does for you. . . .* ***Rule keeping does not naturally evolve into living by faith, but only perpetuates itself in more and more rule keeping, a fact observed in Scripture: 'The one who does these things (rule keeping) continues to live by them.***'"

The purpose of the Law's rule keeping was to keep sinful mankind aware of their propensity to make wrong choices until the Promise would come. Until mankind was finally ready to respond to God in faith alone (a most abstract principle to the hardheaded soul), man was given the Law to help him understand what he needed to do to avoid going to hell. Rule keeping could not save man, only a divine mediator between mankind and God, Jesus Christ, could save man from the consequences of the wrong choices made by his unsurrendered soul.

Just Too Simple

The binding and loosing keys of the Kingdom prayer principles in *Shattering Your Strongholds* appear to many to be just too simple. The unsurrendered soul of the born again Christian fights this simplicity, for the principles of the keys of the Kingdom allow <u>no room</u> for self-preening (which the soul loves) for adhering to any religious regulations that would "make" you holy. Nor do the keys of the Kingdom prayer principles of surrendering everything to God allow for awards to be handed out for gritting-your-teeth acts of the self-will to overcome life's hardest things and turn them into worldly success.

The soul has no interest in anything that does not recognize all it has been through and all it has accomplished on its own. It wants credit for pressing on despite all hurdles, for taking desperately heroic measures to overcome every thing anyone has ever thrown at it. The soul also expects appropriate sympathy, praise, and compensation for having done so. To give God all of the credit is completely unappealing to the soul. To surrender its accumulated baggage and all rights to applause for having carried it so long is not acceptable to the unsurrendered soul, either. And terrifying to the soul is the fact that these keys can strip it of all of the games that keep it on the throne of your life.

People often say, "I've been through years of counseling, Bible studies, conferences, groups, and nothing has healed me yet. I can't believe freedom through Christ and these keys could truly be this simple. Do I really just need to pray and bind my will to the will of God and loose wrong patterns of thinking to start the process? How can it be this easy?" Becoming whole is so easy, so simple, that I even catch myself sometimes furtively looking for hidden trap doors in the binding and loosing principles. There just aren't any.

The well-known acronym K.I.S.S. could easily have stood for Christ's simplest directive to His body: "**K**(eep) **I**(t) **S**(imple), **S**(aint)!" The Good News, the Gospel of Jesus Christ, really is so uncomplicated. Since I believe this, why have I put so many Greek and Hebrew word studies, research information from the classics of Christian faith, and other somewhat "important" quotations into these three books? Certainly not to try to impress you or further complicate the Gospel for you, rather to make you feel more secure about cutting loose the unnecessary, unusable, unbelievably unlivable clutter you have accumulated over your entire life—especially all of the Christian cliches and the humanistic "theological" half-truths you've learned about God.

Your Soul's Salvation

The keys of the Kingdom will simplify your destiny directives by clearing everything out of your mind's record-keeping system that will not enhance your end-times-messenger assignment from God. No, you won't develop holy amnesia—but the neutralized facts of your past will be archived to the way-back-there shelves of your brain where they belong. You have been born into these last days of the Church age for a specific purpose, you know. You have a unique destiny assignment for these times that surpasses anything you have ever thought you might do for God. This assignment is not a Mission Impossible—it is a Mission Totally Possible from heaven's headquarters! The launching of it is just temporarily held up waiting for you to voluntarily strip yourself of the soulish baggage that is hindering you from fulfilling it! Using these Master keys will enhance whatever you are already doing right while revealing whatever you are doing that could be done more effectively. That is a win-win situation, is it not?

Breaking the Power, released in 1997, went deeper into the understanding of the tripartite being of man's body, soul, and spirit. When you accept Jesus Christ as your Lord and Master, the only part of you that gets "saved" or put in spiritual order with God <u>is your spirit</u>. The blood of Jesus Christ created the bridge for you to be drawn into full spiritual communion with your heavenly Father. This connection was the first step to preparing you to live in the full expression of potential that God has always planned for your life.

Step two is the beginning of your understanding that your soul needs healing and cleansing and renewal, a work that you are going to have to agree with, cooperate with, and help punch through! Even though your spirit has been linked up with the Spirit of the Creator of the universe and beyond, your soul still needs to undergo a surrendering of its will, a renewing of its mind, and a healing for its emotions. Important note: God will not fight you for the right to renew your soul from a lifetime of stinkin' thinkin' and old baggage. He will work with you, however, to empower you to voluntarily receive His renewal. You have to clean out the storage lockers of your soul *yourself* to make room to receive it.

Paul wrote in Philippians (2:12), *"Therefore, my dear friends, as you have always obeyed—not only in my presence, but now much more in my absence— continue to work out your salvation with fear and trembling"* (NIV). This is the salvation of your soul!

Christ has done His part, but there is a part of the salvation process that is yours. Your part only requires that you surrender everything you now know about your life.

Matthew Henry's Commentary says this about Philippians 2:12: "(Paul) exhorts them (the Philippian Christians) to diligence and seriousness in the Christian course: Work out your own salvation. . . . It concerns us above all things to secure the welfare of our souls: whatever becomes of other things, let us take care of our best interests. It is our own salvation, the salvation of our own souls. It is not for us to judge other people; we have enough to do to look to ourselves; and, though we must promote the common salvation as much as we can, yet we must upon no account neglect our own. We are required to work out our salvation, *katergazesthe*. The word signifies working thoroughly at a thing, and taking true pains. Observe: we must be diligent in the use of all the means which conduce to our (soul's) salvation . . . . With fear and trembling, that is, with great care and circumspection: Trembling for fear lest you miscarry and come short" (from Matthew Henry's Commentary).

Nowhere does the Apostle Paul or Matthew Henry or any other great saint who truly understood the crucified life—the surrendered soul—ever give allowance for blaming moral shortcomings, miscarriages of will, or any other human failing upon the devil. Nor do they offer reasons for blaming your parents or any of your ancestors. The condition of our souls today is the consequence of all of the wrong choices we have made throughout our lives in addition to our souls' refusal of all personal accountability for having made them.

Yes, things have been done to you, said to you,

and taken from you—no one can deny that. But the condition of your soul today is not the product of those things. Your soul's condition today is the result of its refusal to let go of its reactions to the things of your past. Your soul actually keeps all of the effects of need, pain, and confusion alive by keeping your worst memories on artificial life support. The devil only takes advantage of the doors of access opened by your soul in its attempts to rationalize, justify, and deny its part in the whole mess.

Paul basically told the Philippian Christians that even though their spirits had received salvation, they were accountable for the salvation of their own souls. He was telling them, as he did others who received his epistles, to surrender their own wills—to search the Word and spend time in prayer to renew their minds—to reject fear and open up the deepest closets of their souls for the healing for their emotions.

Divine Plan for Divine Destiny

This divine plan as revealed by the Apostle Paul has not changed from then to now—it is exactly what each one of God's children needs today. Too many think God will imprint His great divine plans for their destinies over the top of their wrong ideas, beliefs, and attitudes and whisk them to victory without any change on their part. He won't. Neither will He scrub out the deception and denial from the inside of your soul if it is resisting a complete abandonment of its throne. Remember, your soul is that unique inner part of you that is yours to hold onto or yours to give over to His plans and purposes for your life. You must make the choice to give it all to Him, holding nothing back. Only then will

He see that the cleansing blood of Christ gets into every nook and cranny of fear, pain, and deception within you.

This does not make a case for His respecting of any divinely sanctioned free will (as further elaborated upon in Chapter Two)—it simply recognizes the incredible power of the human soul to write its own glorious or gruesome future in eternity. Your unsurrendered soul's desire to control and run things must be shattered, smashed, and collapsed—completely. Your soul is meant to fulfill an enormous role in your destiny as an end times messenger, the role of a servant vehicle to manifest God's purposes through your life. It has been created and designed (when it is surrendered) to be the interpreter or translator to the world of what your spirit receives from the Spirit of God. Mercy, now isn't that an incredible function to entrust to such a rascal as the human soul?

What keeps your soul from surrendering to such a divine destiny? The old nature, the sin nature, the old man, the carnal man, the carnal mind—all one and the same. The old nature must be eradicated from your soul which can be accomplished by loosing its self-anointed and self-appointed agendas of what it is determined to do or not do (at any cost). So many people tell me in January that they have surrendered everything to God, and then in February their souls are in a full scale rebellion against God's chastisement of their wrong attitudes and personal agendas that still remain. Never forget that it only takes one tiny seed of rebellion and resistance left in your soul to cause the entire bramble patch to grow back.

As His children, most of us have but a faint resemblance to His true nature—with only an extremely pale likeness of some of His attributes. Unfortunately, however, we have all acquired extremely close likenesses of undesirable attributes from sources other than God—particularly the unsurrendered soulish attitudes and teachings of many of the authority figures of our lives. We must not try to understand God through the attributes of our families, whether natural or the family of God, for even His strongest men and women can upset or disappoint us.

One Master Note

There is so much fussiness towards each other in the body of Christ, it seems difficult to believe we will ever all rise up in unity into the full stature of Christ. Without this unity, we are like arms and legs all pursuing their own agendas, twitching and jerking as we try to walk out our collective earthly destinies. When any human body has had a personal power outage or has cut off links to the power circuits coming from the head, its members become spastic or paralyzed. As members of His Church, the destiny of the world is linked to our ability to share the power circuits coming from our head, Jesus Christ. This multi-sharing requires right agreement with the will of God. Until we as individuals are capable of being in unity in our own individual bodies, souls, and spirits, we are unable to understand this corporate multi-sharing of His power and revelation. If we cannot even get our own personal troops into unity within our own lives, how can we ever get in unity with the rest of body of Christ?

Simply seeking agreement with each other is not the most direct route to unity—the most direct path is seeking to bring all of our wills into agreement with God's will. There has to be one will in charge. This is why choir directors have a single note struck or pitched so the choir can all begin to sing their parts in unity with that one note. There must be a clear Master note for the body of Christ to start out on so everyone can achieve harmonious unity with divine purposes: that Master note is God's will. His will alone is the will to be pursued. Period!

I pray that this book will cause you to see beyond the fussiness of the self-absorbed souls we all have. God's plans and purposes for our lives are so much bigger and higher than our tiny personal agendas and soulish desires. We must look beyond each others' failings and encourage and support everyone to succeed. We must look beyond our own failures and seek God's support to succeed. We must see ourselves and each other as God sees us and press on together towards our united potential.

Those of us who should be fathers and mothers in the faith must grow up and start parenting those who are less mature. Who wants to see fathers and mothers running around with dirty pants and runny noses? Instead of spiritual parents, we have too many adult juvenile delinquents in the body of Christ today— Christians who are seriously delinquent in their spiritual growth and making excuses for it. Mature Christian role models are fine for immature Christians to pattern their understanding after while they are learning how to walk as children of God, pray effectively, and fellowship with other believers. But as we mature, our goal must be to look to Jesus Christ as our role model. Making this transition can become a real power struggle if you do not pull the plug on your soul's internal power source. (I know, I know, mixed metaphors. But having fun with metaphors is one of the few perks of the long, lonely work of writing a book.) The keys of the Kingdom, binding and loosing used upon your own unsurrendered soul, will cut the power cords of your human nature with its limited finite thinking.

Are you willing to at least try these principles of binding and loosing prayers? All you will lose is a little time and a lot of old stuff you don't need anymore. What you can receive is beyond your human comprehension. Just do it and see! It works!

1

It's Time To Grow Up

A First Time Look at the Keys

In Matthew 16:19, Jesus Christ said to His Church, *"I will give unto thee the keys of the kingdom of heaven: and whatsoever thou shalt bind on earth shall be bound in heaven: and whatsoever thou shalt loose on earth shall be loosed in heaven"* (KJV). This important promise is still extended through today.

I had heard so many teachings on these "keys" since I became a Christian in early 1972. I didn't understand all of them and didn't really believe the ones I thought I did understand. Then God began to reveal an entirely new side of these keys to me in 1985. I didn't cooperate with Him as freely as I should have, for I kept wanting others to also understand what God seemed to be telling me. No one did, and I did not want to be alone on what promised to be a rocky road to walk with information that went against so much of what the church world was teaching.

I'm still not certain why God chose me to record and teach this message, except I am very stubborn about what I believe He has said. God has had to really work on me to let go of a lot of half-truths He didn't say during the first 20 of my 28 years as a Christian. I was equal-opportunity stubborn about them, too—but what has remained (even if I go back from time to time to my research to be sure), I now stand upon.

A Promise

In the mid-80s, only one lone friend 200 miles away wanted to hear about this new understanding of Matthew 16:19, Marian Johnson (now on my ministry's Board of Directors). No one else was willing to consider that the keys of binding and loosing might be used in a more effective manner than had already been taught for years. Marian and I prayed together so often by long distance, my phone was turned off when I couldn't pay the bill. Fortunately, my own use of these keys of the Kingdom helped me clear out a heavenly line from God, and His long-distance rates are divinely affordable!

In the early 80s I was just beginning to understand that when a scriptural promise does not seem to materialize in our lives, it might be because we are not where we are supposed to be. Suppose a producer sent you a front row seat pass to his Broadway hit in New York City. The pass was yours, with full promise of a front row seat to this sold-out, smashingly successful new play. Not believing you really had to go to New York to use the pass, you went to the more convenient and closer Mann's Chinese Theatre in Los Angeles instead. You kept going back to Mann's Chinese Theatre for years, but you were never able to receive a front row seat for anything with your pass. You were in the wrong place.

Hear this: The promise of that pass was not broken. Your choice of convenience positioned you in the wrong place to step into the manifestation of its promise. Because of not understanding this truth, many believers have learned to distrust God's big "promises." We have also allowed ourselves to be hindered in believing the promises of God because we have had promises broken by people who have been very important to us. We must never transfer our disappointment in humans to God! God is not a bigger human being, a larger authority figure in our lives. God is God, and He does not break His promises; nor will He ever trick or deceive us. He is for us, not against us—He wants us to succeed! Isn't that great?

Then Who Is Keeping Me Out of the Good Life?

Whether it is large and "out there" with banners flying, or it is sneaky and small like a termite chewing methodically away at your foundation, it is your unsurrendered soul's resistance to the will of God that keeps you out of the good works, the good paths, and the good life that has always been preordained and set in heaven for you. In Ephesians 2:10 (AMP), Paul says, *"We are God's (own) handiwork (His workmanship), recreated in Christ Jesus, (born anew) that we may do those good works which God predestined (planned beforehand) for us, (taking paths which He prepared ahead of time) that we should walk in them—living the good life which He prearranged and made ready for us*

3

to live." His way is the only way for true fulfillment, joy, and excitement beyond what you can handle! How sad it is that we have allowed the razzle-dazzle of the world to make fulfillment, joy, and excitement in the Lord sound dull.

As I travel all across America, I am never bored and never in a rut, because I never know what is going to be around the next corner. I truly do have more excitement in my life every week than I am capable of processing in a conservative manner. So, sometimes I just have to let some of it blow off in private or I could get really silly in public. At these times I dance around my house telling God how much I love Him, my life, my family, my ministry, my house, my car, my cell phone, my blue suit, my white sweater, my frosted-by-God hair, my health, my height, and whatever else pops into my partying soul and spirit! When those two get into agreement to party, you know you're at a party! I don't have to say, "You bless the Lord, O my soul, you bless Him with all that is within you," for my soul is way ahead of that! The best part of this kind of partying is that none of it has any lingering aftereffects to cause me remorse, loss, grief, headaches, or groggy thoughts the next day.

I wish I could always keep my soul in the frame of reference where my spirit lives. But, unfortunately it soon becomes distracted by something or someone and tries to sneak back to its own agendas. My soul has a very short attention span where spiritual things are involved, but that is changing every day. So I again bind my mind, will, and emotions to God to begin to get it back into the partying mode. I can almost always do this early in the morning before my soul has had a chance to get out and bang into the souls of others

4

during the day. It can become harder to pull the partying off once the afternoon begins to roll around.

No matter what kind of an alternative plan your soul's agenda contains, it can never meet your deepest needs, heal your oldest hurts, or answer your most troubling questions and unresolved issues. Your soul's own answers and plans for fulfilling the emptiness of itself will only make you feel more unsettled and empty when the lights go off and the music stops. And your ongoing need, pain, and confusion will make you vulnerable to manipulation by <u>those</u> who know exactly how to use those areas of vulnerability to advance their personal agendas. There are many people who do, and their number is increasing rapidly in these last days as people are learning how to tap into their own soul power!

It's Not Too Late

Do you sometimes worry that your life's problems have taken you beyond the realm of God restoring you to the plans and purposes He has always had for your earthly destiny? That just isn't true! There is great hope for the most unsettled, unsure, neediest, hurting, confused, awkwardly stumbling lamb of God! The Christian who still struggles with bad thoughts, anger, spitefulness, temptation (sometimes losing the fight), failing the Lord's commands, yet who still stumbles back to the Cross in repentance, is loved by God. This confused lamb is as accepted and divinely loved by God as the apostles, the disciples, Charles Finney, and Kathryn Kuhlman were, and as Billy Graham is. Miserable, perhaps—but accepted and divinely loved for sure!

The above saints somehow recognized that it was smarter to quit wrestling with the lure of the world's lights and the desires of their souls and surrender everything they had to God's plans for their lives. That meant constantly challenging their souls' every attempt to derail and sidetrack their destinies. We all have to wrestle with our souls. I don't know if some of us ever will get them 100 percent surrendered here on earth <u>in time</u> to enjoy any great length of freedom and power in our earthly walk. But the BIG NEWS is this: <u>no matter how our souls wage war against us, our born again spirits are just fine</u>!

When you accepted Jesus Christ as your Savior, His blood created the bridge for your unregenerated spirit to be divinely linked to the Spirit of its Creator. This causes the born again spirit to rejoice and want to give all to Christ, without reserve. Such a radical proposal makes the unsurrendered soul very nervous. Its life plan is to hang on to everything it can that might be useful to it some day—to keep records on the names, addresses, and phone numbers of every person it wants to eventually get even with. This is the conflict of your Christianity, saint—the battle between the old nature of the unsurrendered soul and the new nature of the born again spirit. The devil only takes advantage of the open doors of access in your soul that have been created by its attempts to defend its resources of control over your life.

Your Spirit is Just Fine

Knowing that my born again spirit is just fine is very comforting to me when my soul is having a brat day; my body is pitching a tantrum for lemon meringue pie, new shoes, and a nap; and God's assignment sheet has just been delivered to me by the Holy Ghost telling me to get packed and get on a plane to Alabama—NOW! To know that my spirit is connected with the Spirit of my Creator (regardless of what the rest of the troops are falling apart over) is something I find very dear and cling tightly to during my Keystone Kops ride to the airport!

Many come up to me after I've taught this understanding of the status of the born again spirit and the "I'm-not-going-there" unsurrendered soul, wanting to make sure they heard me right. They struggle to grasp that no matter how bad your soul and body might be acting up, if you have accepted Christ as your Savior, your born again spirit is just fine. I don't really believe in eternal security—once saved always saved no matter what you do—but I'm closer in thinking to those who do than I used to be. I believe that our security in Christ is much greater than our ability to sin. What kind of a Savior would He be if our goofiness, our lack of understanding, and our ignorance of His ways could jettison us out of His hands at any time?

If you believe that this could happen, how hard it must be for you to relax in any kind of security about your relationship to the Father. Remember, regardless of how insecure your relationship might have been with your earthly parents, never allow your soul to transfer its insecurities and lack of trust to your heavenly Father who is Almighty God.

However, a human soul that resists repeated dealings of the Lord, consistently rejecting His offer of grace to be set free from the bondage of sin and offenses, is in grave danger. There has to be a point where years and years of this kind of rejection and rebellion against

God's extended grace and mercy and love becomes hardwired into a person's soul to such a degree that they do eventually get themselves eternally lost. But I believe this is so hard to accomplish—that it is so difficult to continue to reject the wooings of the greatest love that ever existed—that most Gospel hardheads simply can't resist Him. To stand in defiance of His grace and mercy and rebel against Him year after year is simply not something many can actually do.

The BIG ISSUE here is not whether or not this could happen—the real issue is that no human being knows at what point it might happen. We must never assume that any have reached that point and cease to believe for their salvation.

I remember my first pastor telling of a carnal Christian who had rejected God's dealings over many years, causing much grief and even the death of a family member. This man was filled with great pride and a strong determination to live his life his way. Several years after having last seen this man, one day the pastor found him sobbing brokenly at the altar. The man's words came through strangled sobs, "I've been so wrong, so wicked, and I've sinned away my day of grace. I'm so sorry now, but I'm lost. God has turned away from me."

The pastor said to him, "My brother, if you had sinned away your day of grace and God had turned from you, your conscience would be seared. You wouldn't care." I believe this to be true. First Timothy 4:1-2 says, in part, *"Now the Spirit speaketh expressly, that in the latter times some shall depart from the faith . . . speaking lies in hypocrisy, having their conscience seared with a hot iron"* (KJV). These verses are speaking of believers who no longer have consciences capable of

8

hearing from God, people who are now lost. The same searing of the conscience can eventually happen to a non-believer as well. But once again, I firmly believe that we humans are completely incapable of determining that inward state of a person's heart from observing any form of that person's outward behavior or attitude.

I am surprised sometimes to find myself invited into super-legalistic religious areas that are so uptight even I have trouble breathing. Here I find the largest number of believers coming to me (frequently in tears), asking if it is <u>really true</u> that they can mess up, repent, blow it again, and still have their born again spirits be right with God? I tell them absolutely. Imagine the condemnation and guilt they have experienced for not conforming to the religious stands they have been taught that born again believers can lose out with God over wrong outward behaviors—wrong behaviors that break their own hearts even as they manifest them.

To Know Him

In Romans 7, Paul laments the struggle he was still experiencing in his walk before God, doing what he did not want to do, not doing what he knew he should do. Yet, God was already using him in mighty ways, proving his apostleship and ministry. God doesn't ask for perfect people, He seeks people who have a genuinely right intent towards Him within their hearts. Paul's intent was to keep growing and learning and serving Christ with everything he could until his earthly death. I don't think Paul was ever satisfied that he had attained all of the fullness of Christ, even though (as he faced his impending death) he said he had fought the good fight, finished the course, and kept the faith (2 Timothy 4:7).

9

Earlier in his epistle to the Christians in Philippi, he said, " *. . . This one thing I do, forgetting those things which are behind, and reaching forth unto those things which are before, I press toward the mark for the prize of the high calling of God in Christ Jesus"* (Philippians 3:13-14, KJV). He expressed over and over that Christ alone was all he really needed—all else in his life was like dung. He said he was forgetting those things which were behind, for he knew he could not press on if he kept dragging them with him. He cut them loose from himself, literally pulling the plug on any artificial life support system his soul tried to sustain them with.

Consider Rahab the harlot. At some point in her life as madam of a whore house, she must have heard one of her customers discussing this God of the Israelites who was killing kings, parting seas, and delivering His people out of Egypt. That ought to tweak your theology about religious and politically correct witnessing! I believe Rahab made a very conscious decision when she heard of this all-powerful God who watched over His people so jealously—that if He ever showed up and would have anything to do with her, she would give her all for Him. I think that God marked her with a big gold "X" at that point, saying, *"See the intent of that heart towards me? Mark her, she's mine!"*

What intrigues me the most about Rahab is that God didn't insist that a deliverance team, the women's ministry council, and the pastor's wife clean her up, enroll her in a discipleship class, and get her a subscription to Christian cable t.v. before He could use her. Upon her heart's decision to seek acceptance from Him, He immediately began to use her—right where she was—to change the course of history and be established as part of the lineage of Christ. He didn't seem to be the least bit concerned about removing her from her surroundings before He had her assist Joshua's men in Jericho. God obviously was more impressed with the inward intent of her soul—which seemingly had turned towards Him in great hope and expectation— than He was in the outward behavior manifested by her physical being.

I am not endorsing wrong behavior here, but far too many Christians judge people (who being restored by God) solely upon their outward actions and appearances. A house designated for restoration is not to be broken apart by a demolition ball and then bulldozed out of the picture because its windows are broken, its paint is ugly, and rats live in its closets! These are symptoms of neglect that need to be fixed. Wrong behaviors existing in a life undergoing divine restoration need to be fixed. They are not symptoms of a salvation that just didn't take! Wrong behaviors in the life of a Christian are symptoms of sources of brokenness and great need being protected by strongholds in the unsurrendered soul. Identifying symptoms without ever addressing their sources is like mopping the floor around an overflowing toilet without ever turning off the water. It gives you something obvious to do, but the cleaning up is never finished.

The church world must stop seeking new and improved ways to manage symptoms and instead direct the body of Christ's attention to the sources of these symptoms. Only then can people get on track with their divine destinies here on earth. The sources are unmet needs, unhealed hurts, and unresolved issues that frightened, angry souls are hiding, protecting, burying, stuffing, coping with, trying to pacify, trying to fix, and trying to chemically blot out—as well as whatever else any soul might believe could effect some form of damage control over the toxic waste within itself. Binding and loosing prayers clear out the smoke screens and stronghold walls in a soul to let God deliver healing to its deepest sources of pain without violating the individual's wounded emotions and battered mental state.

Just Try It

Christians today need to at least try using the keys of the Kingdom, binding and loosing, on the defense systems of their unsurrendered souls. Christians also need to consider a paradigm shift in thinking about the off-kilter spiritual warfare emphasis so many churches and ministries are pursuing today. We must learn to redirect our energies in the most influential manner possible. This requires us to get out of the cycle of fighting fights we don't have to fight with unclean spirits for our own personal victory and begin doing damage to the forces of darkness in high places over our land (see Chapter Nine for more information on this). The body of Christ needs healing within itself to do this effectively.

A former pastor of mine once said, "You can't give what you don't have." How can you impart healing to someone else if you don't have enough faith and confidence in the goodness of God to voluntarily open up your own unhealed wounds and unmet needs to Him? How can you teach others that Christ's forgiveness covers every sin they have ever committed if His forgiveness is not real enough to you to forgive those who have hurt you the most? If we are not healed, if we do not believe Christ's sacrifice was enough to fix every need and wound we have, how will we ever see above our own pain and fear to catch the bigger vision of God's eternal purposes?

We must stop having a caterpillar mentality and realize that our new birth was like a coming out of a cocoon with wings to soar into the heavenlies. I know this is a rather strange metaphor to use for warriors of the faith—just trying to imagine warrior butterflies makes me smile! But the metamorphosis from the old creature to the new creature in God's heavenly realm is just like the grubby ugly caterpillar becoming a beautiful flying creature of the air.

We need to stop searching the Word for personal comfort, personal promises, and personal reassurance that we're going to make it. We can become totally dependent upon the warm milk we find in some of the comfort verses when we should also be chewing up the meat verses of surrender, obedience, forgetting what is behind, and getting on with our destinies. You will not fulfill your destiny tucked away in a Christian crib with a warm bottle. This is okay when you're very young in the Lord, but it is repulsive when it is time that you should be eating meat. Paul said in Hebrews 5:12-14, *"In fact, though by this time you ought to be teachers, you need someone to teach you the elementary truths of God's word all over again. You need milk, not solid food! Anyone who lives on milk, being still an infant, is not acquainted with the teaching about righteousness. But solid food is for the mature, who by constant use have trained themselves to distinguish good from evil"* (NIV).

Note that the above verses say that meat eating believers train themselves to distinguish good from evil by constant use of the nourishment of the meat of the Word. Constant use!

The First Step

We must finally let go of all of our personal self-lists and self-agendas and turn to the Scriptures that promise to involve us in the destiny of nations. We need to stop reacting, accusing, and fussing over who said what and turn fully towards God's ultimate battle plan for the healing of our land. That battle plans reads like this: *"__If My people__ who are called by My name will __humble themselves__, and __pray__ and __seek My face__, and __turn from their wicked ways__, then I will hear from heaven, and will forgive their sin and heal their land"* (2 Chronicles 7:14, NKJ). Did you know that wicked ways include unforgiveness, anger towards others, irritability, seeking of revenge, backbiting, sowing strife and division among the brethren, gossiping in the form of "prayer requests," withholding comfort and encouragement from those who have offended you, and then rationalizing and justifying having done so? Ouch!

This book is about the final adjustments we all need to make to walk forward, no—to march forth in the Spirit. Consider carefully that the prayer principles herein have been proven over and over by many from around the world. The report I hear most often is: "These principles work! They really work!" The first step is to get all of the freedom, strength, healing, and understanding from the Lord that you can. This is not as hard as you think. Understanding and acting upon the gift Jesus has given to us of the keys of binding and loosing is an excellent place to start: *"I will give you the keys of the kingdom of heaven; whatever you bind on earth will be bound in heaven, and whatever you loose on earth will be loosed in heaven"* (Matthew 16:19, NIV).

Jesus knew that when His followers would finally come to Him for forgiveness and healing and help, they would be in an extremely flawed human condition. These specific Kingdom "keys" of binding and loosing will sever bondages and burdens from human lives, but using them is the believer's choice. Believers can choose to use the key of binding to bind themselves to the Kingdom pattern of God's will as it has been set in heaven for them. Believers can choose to use the key of loosing to sever their unsurrendered souls' hold on the accumulation of the unmet needs, unhealed hurts, and unresolved issues of their lives.

Do you think no one knows how much you've been through? Jesus experienced the same things any of us would ever experience in our lives, for He became just like us—a mortal human being on earth. He made himself subject to experiencing all of the human ills, woes, troubles, betrayals, rejections, and hurts that humans know. He was able to do this with surety and grace because He knew God's final plans were for good and not for evil (see Jeremiah 29:11). Jesus was always looking forward to the Father's promise that lay before Him and His followers—a great future on earth and in eternity.

He believed whatever His Father spoke to Him (the Holy Spirit communicating through His "human" spirit) was absolute, completely final, and forever settled TRUTH. Hard as it seems to believe at times, that is all the Father has asked us to do: believe what He says is settled truth. He has said He will take care of all the details.

Jesus Christ never called upon His divine rights (assured by His heavenly position as part of the divine Trinity) to get Him out of anything He faced here on earth. If that had been an acceptable option, why didn't He use His divinity to get out of agonizing in the Garden of Gethsemane or dying upon the Cross of Calvary? He knew that the Father's will was that He would walk this earth just like us, dependent upon listening for the Father's voice and heeding the direction of the Father's Spirit. In so doing, He proved beyond a shadow of a doubt that true victory can be walked out in the center of the human experience on earth. Jesus' promise is that His victorious life in us will make us victorious, too. Just as soon as we get out of His way!

Jesus knew it would be difficult for you and me to make an instant leap of faith to the Father's promise to provide everything we need after we surrendered our lives to Him. We've all been painfully taught by life's experiences that promises are often made with good intention, but later broken when situational factors change. After lifetimes of disappointments, misunder-standings, and betrayal by people we have desperately wanted to believe and trust in, it's not an easy thing to suddenly believe there really is One whose promises are never broken—regardless of situational factors. We have all been conditioned by the world to look out for number one, protecting and defending what we are sure no one else will. So Jesus has basically said, *"I know where you are, and I'm giving you divine Master keys that will open every chained door in your heart so I can be in there with you—to heal your deepest hurts, darkest secrets, and worst pain and shame. These keys will unlock all chains of fear and bondage and set you free to receive, to be, and to do all I have planned for you. Then you will fulfill your earthly destiny—which is to gloriously finish the work I left on earth for you to do when I went back to the Father."*

Jesus Christ also knew that our souls fight to protect (by building personal inner strongholds) much of the ungodly input we have made into our personal "life truths." According to Thayer's Greek/English Lexicon, the strongholds of 2 Corinthians 10:3-5 are arguments and reasonings (excuses) our souls use to fortify and defend our beliefs, regardless of whether they are right or wrong. Personal inner strongholds protect your excuses for why you can't give up an addiction, a wrong belief, a wrong attitude, or a wrong pattern of thinking, as well as why you are fearful. Personal inner strongholds protect the excuses you make for why you believe you will be poor or sick all your life. Strongholds protect the excuses we make for why we are "the way we are," why we know we can't change, and why we blame others for our plight.

To go on, to go through, to go forward in your life can require the cooperation of your will. Your soul can convince you that your will wants to press on, step out, and walk destiny paths with God, while it is actually relying upon your mind to bring up old memories to cause you to retreat from taking such unknown risks. What an internal paradox! This is why it is so good to bind your will to the powerful will of the Father. The Father's will always goes on and goes through. He is always moving forward.

Hands On Revelation

This is strictly a "hands on" revelation understanding. Until you act on these principles, they will always be second-hand knowledge to you. Second-hand revelation can get you out of a few little tight scrapes, but it won't get you out of the big stuff. You need to have <u>first-hand, "been there—done that," experiential, spiritual understanding of your own</u> to successfully deal with the big stuff! You need to absolutely know that the protection, mercy, grace, power, and blessings of God are on you as you totally uproot your known life and set out upon an unfettered adventure with God.

Jesus gave us a prescription for blessing in the Beatitude of Matthew 5:3, *"Blessed are the poor in spirit for theirs is the kingdom of heaven"* (KJV). The word *spirit* as used here is one reason the casual Bible reader can confuse certain things in the Word. Spirit, heart, and flesh do not always mean what you might think they mean in the Scriptures. These three words frequently mean the human soul—the mind, will, and emotions. In Matthew 5:3, the word *spirit* does mean soul according to the detailed breakdown of Thayers Greek/English Lexicon's various definitions of *pneuma* (Strong's/Thayers #4151:2, pnyoo'-mah). The word poor as used here comes from the Greek word *ptochos* (Strong's/Thayers #4434, pto-khos') meaning consciousness of spiritual need. I once read that the use of *ptochos* in this verse means a chosen poverty, a voluntary emptying out of all personal desires, agendas, preconceived ideas, and mindsets in order to receive from God. That makes sense. Those who voluntarily choose to empty themselves of personal agendas and preconceived ideas about God will become very conscious of their spiritual need for Christ. They will be blessed—the Kingdom of heaven shall be theirs.

That's what the Bible says. The world says, "You're not doing well enough, you're not getting all you can. Hey, you only go around once, so you better grab all you can get." The world says, "You need to be more self-assertive so no one pushes you around and takes what you already have."

Garfield the Cat

I received some inspiration on this one day from reading the Garfield the cat comic strip. Garfield is always picking up a newspaper and whacking the same poor spider. In this particular comic strip Garfield walks into view just as the spider comes crawling across the table. Garfield raises his paw to swat it and the spider yells, "You don't scare me, you big hairball!" Garfield blinks and then bops the spider pretty hard. The poor spider ends up with legs bent in every direction.

So what does the spider do? He yells something like, "Is that the best you can do, you mangy pile of fur? I could take you with six legs tied behind my back!" Garfield pulls out a rolled-up newspaper and really clobbers the spider. The poor spider now looks like roadkill. As he's lying there in a pile of tangled limbs, another spider comes across the table and asks, "Harvey, what happened to you?"

Harvey the spider says, "I'm not sure. But I do know that I'm going to get my money back from that self-assertiveness training course I took!" Revelation flash here: Self-assertiveness training can make you stupid!

Prophetic Words and Visions

People sometimes ask me to pray with them to bind a prophecy, a vision, or a word of revelation to them so they can move into the fulfillment of it. I never agree to this. A prophetic word/vision/dream can be misinterpreted if the soul of the individual is still filled with unmet needs and unhealed hurts. A promise in the Bible can be misleading when the person who is trying to appropriate it is not willing to change in order to be mature enough to receive the answer.

In ministering to "Steve," who had been standing on and claiming a prophetic word for nearly six years, I first offered this counsel and then prayed for him: "Steve, that prophetic word given to you may have been directly from God, or it may have been out of the good intent of someone else's love and concern for you. I don't know which it was, so I cannot bind you to the prophecy or bind the prophetic word to you. But here is what I can do—pray for you."

Lord, your timing is always more <u>*right now*</u> *than we realize, but you need to position us and others in order to release aspects of the circumstances that will cause your Word to be fulfilled in our lives. I bind to your will the wills of every person involved in the positioning of Steve in his end times destiny. I bind Steve to your will and purposes for his life, and I bind his mind to the mind of Christ. I bind his hands to the work you've always ordained for him to do, and I bind his feet to the paths you have always ordained for him to walk in these last days.*

Lord, whether this word was or wasn't from you, I bind Steve to your will concerning the end result of it. I loose the effects and influences of any wrong agreements he may have come into regarding its meaning. If the prophecy was from you, Lord, then I ask that you prepare Steve for the unfolding of its outcome. I loose all negative words spoken to him or about him, and I loose any layers of self-defense he has built regarding criticism over this prophetic word.

If the prophecy was not from you, then I ask that you prepare Steve to recognize that and surrender it to you speedily so he can get on into your true plans for his life. I ask that you pour grace and mercy into him so he will relinquish his stronghold thinking about having held onto a false prophecy for so long. I join with him to loose all wrong desires, wrong beliefs, and wrong patterns of thinking about the prophecy or the person who prophesied it to him. Lord, help Steve understand that anyone can prophesy something to us, but that prophecy in itself does not require acceptance and action unless it is from you.

Teach us how to seek the witness of your Spirit on all things that we are told are from you. Lord, help Steve realize that all too often the devil knows exactly what kind of confirmations we will look for (because he is so aware of what we still react to), making sure we find those that will lead us away from God's plans and purposes. I loose every lingering influence from any wrong agreement Steve might have come into. I ask that you set Steve's feet upon the good paths towards the good works you have always planned for him to do for you, showing him how to move speedily into the good life you have always intended him to live. I thank you for Steve, I thank you for his good future, and I thank you for your love and your mercy. Amen.

Slowing Down to Catch Up to God

When God's presence was initially manifested to the Israelites in the desert, they moved when it moved, and they stayed when it stayed. They didn't convene committee meetings, go to counselors, seek out prophetic ministries, or hire church consultants. Today, that cloud of His presence is not visible to the natural eye of mankind. We who are believers must slow down the pace of our lives, shut out the distractions of the world, stay our thoughts upon Christ, review the promises of the Word, and praise Him while we pray. Slowing down with Him always seems to be more productive and get you further faster than speeding up to try to find Him.

I have always been intrigued by the hidden picture within the picture on the three-dimensional posters. You can be told what the "hidden" picture is in the poster and still not see it. I was very frustrated with my inability to discern such pictures at first, and so I tried harder and harder to focus upon finding them. Someone said to me, "Relax and let your eyes go out of focus, then you will be able to see it." That did not make sense to the logic of my mind—my stubborn, do-it-the-way-I-think-best mind. But finally, after a truly frustrating time of trying to make the picture appear to me, I relaxed and let my eyes go slightly out of focus. The hidden picture literally "popped" into view. I couldn't believe how I had missed it. Once I had seen it, even if I looked away, I could always return my gaze to the poster and bring the hidden picture right back into focus.

Many times it is like that with God. We try so hard to focus on what He seems to be hiding from us, or what we just don't get the point of, when we just need to relax. We need to focus on Him, and let what seems to be eluding us go out of focus. We need to be seeking Him first and foremost, and then all that we need will be shown to us (Matthew 6:33). I believe that once the Holy Ghost shows you God's picture for your destiny, even if you are suddenly overwhelmed with life in the fast lane, if you relax and let the focus of your soul's determination soften just a little, God's picture will always pop right back into view. The most important thing here is when He shows you the picture of what to do—then do it!

Cooperating With Him

Cooperating with God means two things to me: 1) Putting off, releasing, laying aside, forgetting those things behind me in order to: 2) Put on, receive, and move forward in relationship with Jesus towards my divine destiny. If we do not take these two steps in this order, our lives can be a futile exercise in trying to cover up smelly old foundation flooring by laying expensive new carpet over the top of it. What is smelly and old and harmful needs to be pried, cut, or ripped out of our souls—not coaxed out, not analyzed out, not rationalized out—but pried, cut, or ripped out.

When a foreign object penetrates your body, such as shard of glass, you can mentally deny it has done so. You can wrap a bandage around it, slather aloe vera over it, or put it in a sling. But a foreign object that does not belong in your body will cause problems. Ruling out the obvious possibility of infection or blood poisoning, there are other complications more subtle. Your physical body begins accommodating the foreign object in your flesh. You may begin limping (favoring a sore foot or leg), using one hand exclusively (favoring a festering sore in the other hand), preferring one part of your body over the rest. The rest of the body is placed into stress by having to pick up and carry the load meant for one specific part.

The baggage of your life is like foreign objects embedded in the flesh of your soul. But getting the baggage out and gone won't happen without a fight from your soul. Isn't that silly? Your soul becomes accustomed to accommodating those foreign objects—even keeping some of them on artificial life support—ever ready to be flashed in your face to control you. Think back to some of the times you thought God was telling you to do something awesome, something bigger than you ever dreamed you could, and you began to think about actually going for it. Suddenly you had a memory flashback of another time when you thought God was telling you to do something and you stepped out and failed.

Your soul begins to question, "Are you sure you really want to go through that again? Do you remember how embarassed you were? Remember how people stopped taking you seriously after that? Are you sure this is what you want to do?" You suddenly get a "revelation" to pull back and just pray for a year before you do this thing for God. Guess what? Your soul got you again. It controlled you by painful and humiliating memories that may not even be true anymore, having been creatively rewritten by your soul during the time that has elapsed since they were birthed.

Consequences

You are the one who makes the choice to continue believing the painful and scary things your soul protects with its stronghold thinking. These stronghold patterns generally won't be removed by thinking, willing, or crying them loose. You need the Kingdom key of loosing to pry, cut and rip them out. Many of the most frightening memories you have are constantly being reinforced by ongoing consequences that seem to keep materializing over and over. This happens when you don't understand how to stop the <u>source</u> of the consequences. I have seen people trying to rebuke or command consequences out of their lives, consequences coming directly from wrong choices they continue to make. You can't command or rebuke consequences out of your way. That's like trying to rebuke your nose. Rebuke it and command it to be gone all you want, it will still be right there in the middle of your face. So will consequences—in your face whichever way you turn.

Some people are so into the denial of their sources of soul distress that they believe God understands and exempts them from obeying parts of His Word. They rationalize that His grace is sufficient to allow them to do so. Wrong! His grace is sufficient for everything in your life, but it will never neutralize the consequences of your disobedience and denial. God sometimes just lifts His grace and lets these consequences ride over you like a herd of elephants. First thing you know, you are back to rebuking and commanding and casting out, trying to get the elephants out of your face. You can't rebuke, cast out, or even loose a consequence (or an elephant, either!) out of your life.

It is much more productive and effective to bind your will to the will of God and bind your mind to the mind of Christ, asking the Holy Spirit to teach you from your consequences. Try to even thank Him for the consequences that will help you learn where you went wrong so you won't do it again. A lesson easily learned can be a lesson easily forgotten. A lesson learned the hard way is much harder to forget. Begin to loose the clouds and the clutter of wrong thought patterns and wrong attitudes that cause you to be unsure of whether or not you can make the right choice the next time. Remember that you can do all things through Jesus Christ who strengthens you (Philippians 4:13). You can make right choices every time when you don't have a lot of wrong, confusing baggage clogging up your soul.

Binding yourself to the will of God and loosing wrong patterns of thinking can make it much easier to go through the school of consequences that you have birthed with wrong choices. You can learn from your wrong choices even as you are cleaning up the consequences and declaring, "I'm not going to do that again!" Did you know that God is never closer than when you are trying to clean up some of the messes of your life? He knows that you are coming nearer to being at the end of yourself where you may finally say, "God, everything I've tried to make life work for me doesn't work anymore! Why have I been doing this to myself and how can I stop?"

God's answer would be, *"You've been depending on the wrong things, and you need to begin depending only on me. You're trying to cope with effects and influences you have held onto from traumatic things that happened to you ten, twenty, even thirty years ago. You're going to have to let them all go and trust me to shake it all out and make it right."*

An elderly lady of ninety-two years calls our ministry periodically and always says the same thing, "Would you pray for me, please? I just cannot get over what my family did to me when I was a little girl." Her pain and shame and blame is so deeply etched into her soul, we still have not been able to pray her through to a victory. But we haven't given up. I often ask people,

"Do you want to be ninety-two and still be processing your stuff, if you're here that long? Or would you like to let it go now and get on with your destiny future?" What do you want?

2

It's Self-Will, Saint, Not Free Will

Challenges From Self-Willed Wills

For most of my Christian walk, I have heard Christians (individuals, ministers, leaders, etc.) say aloud: "God has given us a free will and He won't cross it," while quite likely thinking to themselves (**and neither will anyone else!**). Is this right to a free will the unspoken eleventh commandment, carved-in-stone—with God saying <u>He shalt not</u>? For years I thought it might be so, but I've changed my mind.

God has given us freedom to make choices with a bottom line responsibility of our then being accountable for having made them. None of us really want to be held responsible for the sometimes far-reaching fallout of our wrong choices—for just like the rain, fallout falls upon the just as well as the unjust. It is time we recognize that the madness of the world is the result of man's determination to consult his own soul for information on his choices, rather than consulting God. God is not to blame for the state of the world today, and the devil has only been taking a free ride on our religious roller coaster.

I believe we must accept that the body of Christ is primarily to blame for the chaos of the world around us today. Why? **Because Christians have always had the answer to reversing the madness**. Second Chronicles 7:14 tells us that God said this, *"If my people, which are called by my name, shall humble themselves, and pray, and seek my face, and turn from their wicked ways; then will I hear from heaven, and will forgive their sin, and will heal their land"* (KJV). Adamantly pursuing our own free wills will always result in wicked ways. Sweetly singing *All to Jesus I surrender, all to Him I freely give,* while denying that we are still holding onto wrong personal beliefs, offenses, unforgiveness, judgementalness, criticalness, and coveteousness is spiritual hypocrisy. This is the result of the self-will's desire to control.

Two Challenges

Ever since *Shattering Your Strongholds* came out, there have been two questions or statements that have continued to surface from time to time by mail, telephone, in person, e-mail, and otherwise: One is: "What makes you think you have any right to bind another Christian's will to the will of God? That's witchcraft! We Christians have a free will, you know, and no one has the right to bind our wills to anything!"

As soon as I hear that phrase, I know I'm hearing from a strong self-willed individual.

The second statement is: "I don't believe you have any right to bind another Christian's mind to the mind of Christ. That's mind control!" Again, I know that I am being addressed by an unsurrendered soul (mind, will, and emotions) in full reactionary mode, a soul that senses a severe challenge to its right to choose what to do and what to think at all times.

I know there are some who are genuinely distressed over my teaching that it is acceptable to bind other peoples' wills to the will of God as well as binding their minds to the mind of Christ. This is the sad result of determined teachings on the sanctity of the Christians' precious free will. These so-called free wills have sent may Christians to the poor house, especially with some of the money scams so many American Christians bought into throughout the church world (from East Coast to the West Coast) in the nineties. How "free" indeed was that exercise of the free will after the costs were considered? Free wills have sent some Christians into an early grave. Free wills have caused calamitous grief to many Christian families. These same free wills have sent many unbelievers, who vehemently fought for their rights to free will choice, to hell.

I can't afford a free will. I am always appreciative of others' prayers for my will to be bound to God's will.

I can find no direct reference to free will in either the Old or New Testament. Christians must stop believing what they find convenient to believe and begin to seek God's perspective on every issue of their walk with Him. Because so many have not done so, people still come up to me in meetings in varying emotional states—some angry, some crying, some sad, some puzzled—asking, "How have we missed this understanding on binding and loosing for so long? Why hasn't this been taught—why haven't we heard this before?"

I simply answer, "I don't know. But you have heard it now. What are you going to do with it?"

I suspect that many are going to struggle with this chapter which states that Christians should expect no rights to retaining their free wills when they surrender themselves to Christ. Think for a moment about what you prayed when you gave your life to Him. I prayed something like this, *"I thank you, Lord, for sending your Son to die for me on the cross so I could be forgiven of my sins. I ask your forgiveness and receive what He has done for me so that I can be free of guilt for all of my past; I now surrender my life to Him. I make you Lord of my life, Jesus."* How can you surrender your life to Him, make Him Lord of your life, and then insist upon the right to choose whether or not to obey His every wish?

Memorable Free Will Mistakes

God created Adam and Eve, the beginning of all mankind, with the ability to make choices. Once Adam and Eve were put out of the Garden for their wrong choices to disobey God's command to not eat of the Tree of Knowledge of Good and Evil, where was their free will choice to return to the Garden? There was none.

Did Lot have a free will choice as to whether or not to flee Sodom and Gomorrah? Genesis 19:15-16

(NAS), *"When morning dawned, the angels urged Lot, saying, 'Up, take your wife and your two daughters, who are here, lest you be swept away in the punishment of the city.' But he (Lot) hesitated. So the men (angels) seized his hand and the hand of his wife and the hands of his two daughters, for the compassion of the LORD (was) upon him; and they brought him out, and put him outside the city."*

Lot might have chosen to remain in the city with his sons-in-law-to-be who refused to believe they were in danger, but God's angels did not allow him any choice. They seized Lot's hand (Hebrew: captured, caught, apprehended, arrested—pretty forceful definitions!), his wife's hand, and the hands of his two daughters and pulled them out of the city. Lot's wife made a self-willed choice to disobey the angels and sneak a little peek back at the city she had lived in, and the price for doing this was very high—her "free will" cost her life.

What about Jonah? The Lord ordered Jonah to go to the city of Ninevah and cry out against the wickedness of its inhabitants. Jonah promptly exercised his free will to run off, board a ship, and head out to sea to get as far away from Ninevah as he could. God raised such a storm about this that the sailors threw Jonah overboard, and he spent three days in the belly of a whale. Jonah could have said, "At least I'm not going to Ninevah!" He would have probably died right there, celebrating his free will. Jonah might have been foolishly disobedient, but he wasn't stupid.

Have you ever felt that your disobedience has deposited you into a situation (i.e. whale belly) that no one can possibly help you get out of? Jonah did. Read what he was thinking in that whale's belly (Jonah 2:4-10, NIV): *"I said, 'I have been banished from your sight; yet I will look again toward your holy temple. The engulfing waters threatened me, the deep surrounded me; seaweed was wrapped around my head. To the roots of the mountains I sank down; the earth beneath barred me in forever. But you brought my life up from the pit, O LORD my God. When my life was ebbing away, I remembered you, LORD, and my prayer rose to you, to your holy temple. Those who cling to worthless idols forfeit the grace that could be theirs. But I, with a song of thanksgiving, will sacrifice to you. What I have vowed I will make good. Salvation comes from the LORD.' And the LORD commanded the fish, and it vomited Jonah onto dry land."*

After Jonah prayed, God <u>commanded</u> that whale to vomit him out onto dry land. What a concept! If God can position a whale on a shoreline of dry land and make it throw up, God can certainly take care of whatever or whoever seems to have you trapped in the consequences of your disobedience! <u>The only catch is: He expects you to realize that He is delivering you to put you back on track with your destiny and His will.</u> Beware of casually walking away from a divine intervention in your direst of circumstances to pursue your life in the same manner that got you into the whale's belly in the first place! God has little patience for that.

I often wonder how some of today's spiritual warfare "experts" deal with the story of Jonah. I heard one deliverance minister say: "Some of the writers of the Old Testament were drinking too much wine when they wrote some of those stories." I almost choked when I heard him say that. One lamb came to me after the meeting and said, "Now I can't help but wonder if some of the New Testament writers were drinking, too." We must never try to rationalize away the parts of God's

Word that do not fit with our preconceived ideas about Him. We must change our perceptions to come into alignment with the reality of His truth.

Paul Moved From Self-Will to Submitted Will

In the book of Acts Paul told King Agrippa how he had exercised his free will to persecute and kill the early Christians. Paul said (Acts 26:11-16 NKJ), *"And I punished them often in every synagogue and compelled them to blaspheme; and being exceedingly enraged against them, I persecuted them even to foreign cities. While thus occupied, as I journeyed to Damascus with authority and commission from the chief priests, at midday, O king, along the road I saw a light from heaven, brighter than the sun, shining around me and those who journeyed with me. And when we all had fallen to the ground, I heard a voice speaking to me and saying in the Hebrew language, 'Saul, Saul, why are you persecuting Me? It is hard for you to kick against the goads.' So I said, 'Who are You, Lord?' And He said, 'I am Jesus, whom you are persecuting. But rise and stand on your feet; for I have appeared to you for this purpose, to make you a minister and a witness both of the things which you have seen and of the things which I will yet reveal to you.'"*

Jesus told Paul that He had appeared to him to make him a minister and a witness. I don't see any place in this passage where Christ told Paul that he had any input into the matter. To truly surrender to the Lordship of Jesus Christ requires us to submit and obey, often with no whys, whens, wheres, or hows allowed.

Power with God requires sacrifice, and your self-will is the sacrificial goat. What if Christ had said, *"If*

35

you need me to die for you, let me know. I will try my best." He didn't try to make the right choice about anything; <u>He just automatically obeyed His Father's will!</u>

The fact that some Christians doggedly insist they have the right to free will choice even with God means they want a back door option available just in case they have to tell God they can't do something He asks. The soul will never willingly give up its right to control even your choice to obey God. Control must be taken from the soul by force, employing the Word, the keys of the Kingdom, the actions of your life, and your commitment to obedience and surrender. Easy? No. Impossible? No. Can anyone do it? Yes, absolutely!

I am fully aware that my free will only caused me trouble and grief, not to mention the trouble and grief it caused so many others. I have told the Lord that I am reaffirming having surrendered my will at the foot of the Cross every time I bind my will to His will. Still, that silly will of mine has a highly developed homing instinct, just like some goofy kind of pigeon, and it keeps trying to get back Soul Control Central. So I keep taking it back to the foot of the Cross again and again, by binding it to His will. I do this believing the Word of the Living Word who assured me that *"Whatsoever I would bind on earth would be bound in heaven"* (Matthew 16:19). There is a time coming—here on earth—when I'll put that dirty bird at the foot of the Cross and it will not get back up!

Here's My Will—Please Take It!

The generally accepted Christian belief that God won't violate our free wills does not prove that He has anointed and appointed us the right to remain self-willed! Personally, if you were to find me on top of a fourteen-story building tomorrow morning, toed up to the edge of the ledge, declaring that by a choice of my free will and my fine mind, I was choosing to dive headfirst into the parking lot below—guess what? You have (in writing right here!) my permission to pick up a brick and take out my free will and fine mind in order to save my life. I consider my right to life in eternity with Christ far more important that my right to make daily choices that should be no choice at all.

The actual phrase *self-will* is found only once in the Old Testament (Genesis 49:6) in a negative and gory verse. The New King James version of Scripture tells us that Jacob spoke final words to all of his sons just prior to his death, saying this about Simeon and Levi (vss. 5-7), *"Simeon and Levi are brothers; instruments of cruelty are in their dwelling place. Let not my soul enter their council; let not my honor be united to their assembly; for in their anger they slew a man, and in their self-will they hamstrung an ox. Cursed be their anger, for it is fierce; and their wrath, for it is cruel! I will divide them in Jacob and scatter them in Israel."*

The phrase *self-will* (human will devoid of divine control) is found twice in the New Testament in the sense of pleasing oneself. The human will placed under divine control happens only when there is a voluntary sacrifice of all pursuits of pleasing oneself. In Titus 1:7 (NAS) we read that one who would be an overseer in spiritual things *" . . . must be above reproach as God's steward, not self-willed, not quick-tempered, not addicted to wine, not pugnacious, not fond of sordid gain."* Second Peter 2:10-11 (NKJ) speaks of *" . . . those who walk according to the flesh in the lust of uncleanness and despise authority. They are*

presumptuous, <u>self-willed</u>. They are not afraid to . . ."
do things that angels (who are ever more stronger and
powerful than we are) would never do. The Greek word
used here for self-willed is described both in Thayers
and Strong's #829 as—*authades*—(ow-thad'-ace),
meaning self-pleasing and arrogant. This is not a place
I want to go, a thing I want to do or be anywhere near.

If God has to pressure you to surrender your free
will to be honest before Him (the sinner's prayer does
include committing your all to Christ as Lord and
Master), His pressuring can get pretty intense. When
He focuses in on the destiny of your life here and in
eternity, He can get **really** focused—just like a white-
hot laser beam. You and I focus on the discomfort of
His focus. The discomfort comes from the tension of
resisting His will—sort of like clamping down onto an
infected tooth that the dentist is trying to separate from
your infected jaw. Ouch, ouch, ouch!

But I Think I'm Okay

It is so easy to rationalize human reasoning and
logic. If my soul wants to do something, it can find
100 reasons why it should and how it can. If my soul
does not want to do something, it can find 100 reasons
why it should not and why it can't. We have a will that
can choose what it wants—but always with
consequences. Consequences are the bump in the night
that shows up after the choice maker (the unsurrendered
soul) pretends to have gone to bed.

There is a basic law of physics that says that two
things cannot occupy the same place at the same time.
That law of physics works for the spiritual realm as
well. All too often we have our soul sitting on the throne

of our lives, spiritualizing everything it can to convince us that God is really sitting on that throne. The Apostle John said, *"He must increase, but I must decrease"* (John 3:30, NKJ). The "I" here is the unsurrendered soul. My soul's involvement in my Christian walk must decrease tremendously before I can have any great increase of His life flowing through me.

Christ Denied His Own Will

Matthew 26:39-43 tells us that Christ asked His Father, in the Garden of Gethsemane, if the terrible circumstance of the death He was facing could be changed. Immediately thereafter He denied His own will and asked for the Father's will to be done. *"Going a little farther, he fell with his face to the ground and prayed, 'My Father, if it is possible, may this cup be taken from me. Yet not as I will, but as you will.' Then he returned to his disciples and found them sleeping. 'Could you men not keep watch with me for one hour?' he asked Peter. 'Watch and pray so that you will not fall into temptation. The spirit is willing, but the body is weak.' He went away a second time and prayed, 'My Father, if it is not possible for this cup to be taken away unless I drink it, may your will be done.' When he came back, he again found them sleeping, because their eyes were heavy"* (NIV).

He had asked His closest friends to come with Him into the Garden as He agonized as a man over what He was facing. They fell asleep when He needed them most. These friends had determined in their souls (their minds, wills, and emotions) that they would not let Him down—yet they did. When Christ said the *spirit* was willing, the original Greek word used here for spirit is *pneuma*

39

(Strong's/Thayers #4151:2—pnyoo'-mah). This particular translation means the power by which a human being feels, thinks, wills, and decides. It was in their souls that the disciples had convinced themselves they would never leave Him, that they were willing to be whatever He needed them to be. In the same verse, we also read that Christ said the *flesh* is weak. The disciples went to sleep which shut down their physical senses of sight and hearing, the very senses that would have heard and seen their Friend agonizing, perhaps transmitting compassionate messages to their souls to go to Him.

The English word *temptation* in this verse has been translated from the Greek word *peirasmos* (Strong's/Thayers #3986:b, pi-ras-mos'), which means a trial of man's fidelity, integrity, virtue, and constancy. The unsurrendered soul is not capable of fidelity, integrity, virtue, and constancy in itself alone. The best of your soul's intentions will fail when things get hard unless it has surrendered to input from the Holy Spirit—input already deposited in and waiting to flow out of your spirit.

It's Your Self-Will Doing All the Fussing

When you are feeling and acting fussy, fearful, and frustrated, you can guarantee that your unsurrendered soul has a solid hold on something it does not want to release. You may have felt sure that you had surrendered a certain thing to Jesus—but the actual surrender of it was only a delusion. Fussiness, fearfulness, and frustration are the feelings of those whose private territory is being threatened by a hostile take over. Your not-yet-fully-renewed mind always sees any invasion of its "No Trespassing" areas as a hostile take over.

Paul tells us in Romans 8:6-8 (KJV), *"To be carnally minded is death; but to be spiritually minded is life and peace. Because the carnal mind is enmity against God: for it is not subject to the law of God, neither indeed can be. So then <u>they that are in the flesh cannot please God.</u>"* Verse 9 goes on to tell us that Paul told the Roman Christians that they were not in the flesh. He was speaking to their both <u>potential and positional</u> new creature status as Christians, which they had not yet fully grasped. Paul was not making a declaration in verse 9 that a Christian could not be in the flesh. It is all too clear in the Church today that this is completely possible. Those who are struggling to escape the carnal ways of their unsurrendered souls end up deciding to do one of three things: 1) condemn themselves for struggling in the first place or 2) rationalize the struggle because of all that's been done to them in the past or 3) deny any struggle while believing they are fully surrendered.

In order to surrender all to Jesus Christ, you are first going to have to resign as the CEO of your life. The word is out, Christian, your soul's job has to be downsized. So tell it to make it easy on itself and you— just prepare its resignation and turn it in! Full surrender to God means you are freed of being responsible for the outcome of your life. Your life becomes the responsibility of Jesus Christ. He becomes the CEO of your formerly non-profitable status and begins to form you into a profitable servant of the Kingdom. He has no problem with being responsible for you, in fact He applied for that job before you were ever born. And, best of all, He is no buck passer!

To give your all to Christ, you must surrender your right to a free will choice every time you see a fork in

41

the road of your Christian walk. You are not going to be able to continue to rationalize what you will be spiritual about, and you will not be allowed to retreat in denial when you are choosing to be soulish about a certain situation or person. You will no longer be able to cloak yourself in the belief that your true agendas and motivations of self are hidden from all view. You will know you must give it all up to Him.

Attitude on Parade

I use what God has shown me about these prayer principles every chance I get. I am always praying some form of the binding and loosing prayers, several times a day and sometimes repeatedly during the night. I bind my mind to the mind of Christ and loose wrong patterns of thinking and wrong ideas out of it because I want to make more room for new revelation to come in. I bind myself to God's will and timing. I bind all of the human factors of circumstances and situations around me to God's will, truth, and timing. I loose all wrong beliefs, ideas, patterns of thinking, attitudes, and otherwise from myself and others, and then I wait for God's will to be manifested. If I don't do the above, I can find myself having to walk out the consequences of my will's wrong choices in the world's harsh timing.

Any time I begin to relax and let my guard down, God will maneuver me into difficult situations or allow the enemy to maneuver difficult people around me to get my attention and reveal that I'm getting sloppy in my attitudes. I fly all over the U.S. to keep ministry commitments, sometimes with very tight schedules between assignments. Probably every major airline in the U.S. has been the target of one of my soulish attitudes at one time or another. I do publicly repent for that here and now (pass it on)!

I've made foolish declarations that I will never fly on this airline or that airline again. When you've decided not to use just about every major airline there is—ever again—eventually you have to rethink your position and start over with some of them. Either that, or get your own private jet. During the months of April and May of 1999, it seemed that United Airlines was out to get me. Every time I turned around, it seemed that one of my United flights was cancelled or delayed, or my luggage went astray, or I lost a traveling companion in the hubbub of rushing from one gate to another in a large airport. I did lose my traveling companion, Evelyn, in Chicago's O'Hare Airport once, being told by a United Airlines gate "keeper" that she was probably already on the plane about to depart to Knoxville TN, and did I want to get on that plane RIGHT NOW or not. I did and she wasn't.

On that particular return flight to California (after several days in Tennessee), with only 15 hours at home in Sacramento to wash clothes, take a shower, and sleep before flying out again, I was told that our United Airlines departure would be delayed once again for an hour due to traffic problems over Chicago. This delay would cause us to miss our connection out of Chicago's O'Hare, with our luggage going who knew where. I began to get upset, realizing even if any lost luggage was actually located and delivered the following day, we were scheduled to fly on to Spokane early the next morning. If our luggage ever caught up to us, it would contain many things that definitely needed washing, sorting, even replacing.

As my soul began to rev up for a real confrontation, I was aware of the Holy Ghost whispering in my ear, *"If you think it's been difficult up 'til now, it's going downhill from here if you don't get your attitude adjusted!"* I knew that this would certainly be true, but I didn't want to adjust my attitude. I was tired, I was overwhelmed with flying right back out early the next morning, and I was not happy with anything—especially United Airlines.

Still, I have used these principles long enough to know that a direct communique delivered like that was a last warning before things began to get really ugly in the natural realm of life. And I was the one who held the keys to choose to keep Door Number Two, the Ugly Door, wide open. So I swallowed a couple of times, turned around and began to walk to my gate where I would sit and wait out the next hour of delay. I bound my mind to the mind of Christ, and I bound my will to the will of God. I bound the minds and wills of every United Airlines employee and Chicago's O'Hare Airport employee to the mind of Christ and the will of God. Then I loosed all of the word curses I'd spoken—or at least thought—about every single one of them! I loosed all of the wrong agreements I'd tried to make with anyone who would listen that United Airlines was out to get me personally. I prayed for God to bless these employees and heal them and comfort them as other soulish attitudes came towards them from other fussy and frustrated passengers.

I was at peace within minutes and relaxed with my book. After finally boarding the plane for Chicago, I was unusually blessed with three open seats in my row. I put the armrests and my feet up, accepted a diet Coke and a snack, and kicked back. When we landed at O'Hare, I was surprised (but not really) to see that our connecting flight had also been held up for an hour. Isn't that a coincidence? Of course it isn't! I believe our particular connecting plane was waiting right there for us is because I had forced my soul to undergo a "key" attitude adjustment. While I might need a refresher course in this truth from time to time, God is always ready to give me a final warning so I can make the right choice. If I refuse to make the right choice, the consequences resulting from that error can seem endless and even vicious. Following is a sample prayer on how to deal with wrong thoughts in your own soul.

Wrong Thought Life

Jesus, the more I bind my mind to your mind, the more aware I become of critical thoughts about others. I choose to recognize this and loose those wrong thoughts. I will refuse to allow my soul to feed upon wrong thoughts to try to overcome its feelings of anger and frustration. My will sometimes pushes so hard towards acting upon the ungodly thoughts in my mind. I confess that I still struggle with wanting to see others pay for the things lodged in my soul, but I know it is your will that my mind be free of anger, bitterness, and complaining. I loose all wrong thoughts, all wrong beliefs, and the effects and influences of all wrong agreements I have entered into over what I have perceived as cruel or just plain inconvenient injustices towards me. I loose the strongholds that my soul has built to justify and rationalize my right to seek agreement about them.

45

Thank you for the keys of the Kingdom which help me come into alignment with your desired plans and purposes. I bind every one of my thoughts to the obedience of Christ (2 Corinthians 10:5). I loose all vain and evil imaginations within my mind, for I will not allow my soul to exalt them between me and you. I ask that you judge every form of my thinking where I may be deceived and then correct me. You have said that I should think on whatever is pure, lovely, admirable, excellent, and praiseworthy. I bind my mind to thoughts patterned after love, patience, and kindness. I will not think envious, boastful, or proud thoughts. I will believe the best of those I need to interact with, and I will hope and believe for good thoughts to come back towards me. I will practice thinking the best of every person I meet, expressing only attitudes of the fruit of the Spirit.

I loose all thoughts of unforgiveness, discouragement, and negativity. I bind my thoughts to your thought patterns, Jesus. Help me to be aware when my thinking patterns begin slipping out of alignment with you. Help me guard my words when I'm struggling for right thought patterns. I love you, Lord, and I am so grateful for your thoughts of good will towards me. Help me remember to always think likewise. Amen.

This prayer helps clean house in the unsurrendered soul. Your soul never wants to throw away anything that rationalizes and justifies its departing from the attitudes of the fruit of the Spirit. It wants to hang on to everything it recognizes as potential excuses for self-willed behavior.

Strongholds, Inc.

Denying that we have selfish, soulish wrong attitudes requires us to justify and rationalize their existence within us. Justifications, rationalizations, excuses, and denial are all building materials of personal, inner strongholds. According to Ephesians 4:27 (AMP), such "construction work" gives the devil room, opportunity, and a foothold in the life of the one doing the constructing (read *Breaking the Power* Chapter Two for further understanding). Such stronghold construction compounds the consequences of any problem, for strongholds open doors of access for evil spirits to pressure and harrass everyone involved. This is unclean spirits' favorite pastime, making things hotter and more uncomfortable for all souls on parade. Demonic spirits just love a parade! Open doors of access in your soul always bring about a lose-lose situation with the devil— as well as giving him opportunities to inflame fear within your soul and to set you up for accidents and illnesses (see Chapter Six on Healing).

When circumstances reach this level of chaos, many desire to believe the devil to be the source of the problem. Not so—the devil is only taking advantage of the problem. What appears to many to be the manifestation of personality traits of an evil spirit is almost always a bad attitude coming out of an unsurrendered soul. Several people involved in deliverance ministries have said to me, "Well, I know what you mean and you know what I mean. You call it a wrong attitude, I call it a spirit. We're both saying the same thing."

I emphatically reply, "No, we are not saying the same thing. An external evil spirit is not the same thing as an internal wrong attitude!" One is spirit and the other is soul, two separate entities. If you can blame a difficult consequence on an evil spirit's actions, then it is not your fault. If you have to blame your own bad attitude for a difficult consequence, then it is your fault. You can rationalize that you are not accountable for the actions of an evil spirit. You cannot honestly rationalize not being accountable for your own bad attitudes. Also, there is always the hope that an evil spirit can be cast out of you. But here is the bottom line—you cannot have a wrong attitude cast out of your unsurrendered soul. It almost always comes down to the fact that you can't be delivered from yourself—you have to deal with yourself!

Caterpillars and Butterflies

The Apostle Paul told the Roman Christians (Romans 12:2, AMP), *"Do not be conformed to this world—this age, fashioned after and adapted to its external, superficial customs. But be transformed (changed) by the (entire) renewal of your mind—by its new ideals and its new attitude—so that you may prove (for yourselves) what is the good and acceptable and perfect will of God, even the thing which is good and acceptable and perfect (in His sight for you)."* Thayers Greek/English Lexicon describes the original Greek word *anakainosis* (Strong's/Thayers #342, an-ak-ah'-ee-no-sis), which is translated here as renewal (renewing, KJV), as meaning a complete change for the better. This same Greek word comes from another word meaning reversal of what was before.

A large majority of Christians today are still hampered by old thinking, by the clinging, rotting grave clothes of their adamic "cocoons." As born again new creatures in Christ, we are to be transformed from our old soulish (carnal) creature to a new spiritual creature in the same manner as the caterpillar undergoes a transformation in his cocoon before he can emerge as a butterfly. This transformation is called metamorphosis. Romans 12:2 (NIV) tells you to be *"transformed by the renewing of your mind."* The original Greek word used for "transformed" is *metamorphoo* (Strong's/ Thayers #3339, met-am-or-fo'-o), meaning to change into another form (to metamorphose).

Years ago I remember hearing an anointed evangelist say, "All things are parallel," meaning that there are parallels between the natural realm and the spiritual realm of life. Identifying some of these parallel happenings can help our natural minds to better understand spiritual things. This is why I tell so many stories when teaching, relating spiritual concepts to natural principles in life. Spiritual concepts can be quite abstract when you think about it. When you are hopelessly entangled in sin and bondage, abstract just doesn't cut it! People in bondage can use natural parables to help them grasp spiritual concepts to get free.

Paraphrasing the Encyclopaedia Britannica's explanation of metamorphosis (by superimposing the parallel of man's natural/spiritual states over the caterpillar/butterfly states), I will do no harm to the facts of its information. I hope to offer a new way to look at the old creature/new creature state with regard to the Christian new birth. Metamorphosis in the animal world is the transformation of an *infant state of being* into a entirely unrecognizable and different state as an adult. This is a process complicated by the degree of difference between the two states of being. I have always been amused by our soulish/spiritual parallel with regard to the caterpillar being a worm-like creature in no way resembling the final state of the glorious, airborne butterfly. We all need to get rid of our grubby, wormy, caterpillar-like attitudes, realizing that no matter how we dress them up, part their hair in the middle, and put red bows and long streamers on them: CATERPILLARS CAN'T FLY. (For those of you who have heard my tapes, this is another CHICKENS CAN'T SWIM analogy!)

The process of the transformation of creatures in the animal world who undergo metamorphosis may be gradual, extending over a long period and involving a number of intermediate stages—or the transformation may be achieved in one step. In the animal world, the creature undergoing the transformation has absolutely nothing to say about any of the process, whether the transformation will be multi-phased or happen in one big swoop. In the latter case, nearly everything about the infant (former, old, etc.) creature state is dissolved and disintegrated at a rather rapid rate.

In the human world, the soulish/spiritual creatures undergoing divine transformation unfortunately have a great deal of latitude in choosing whether to rebel vehemently at any stage, submit just a little when things seem to look promising, or completely abandon themselves to the transforming process. The difference in the transformation from the old creature into the new creature in Christ is so profound that nothing, not even a teeny pinch, of the original functions of the infant state are of any value to the new creature. In the natural realm of metamorphosis, the old creature often has to be completely dissolved and then restructured into a totally new creature with no resemblance at all to its former state of being. So that no changes are made prematurely and no necessary systems are left behind in the general transformation from one natural creature state to another, there is an all-encompassing signal for the change to begin. The signal is a hormonal one sent in the blood to all the cells and tissues of the creature's body, a signal that says there is to be a total withdrawal of the juvenile hormone RIGHT NOW.

So many Christians who should have long since moved way beyond their infant state of spiritual growth sometimes find themselves at such a loss as to why their soul's comfort zone no longer seems to be available to them. When that happens, I think God has withdrawn the baby-Christian juvenile hormone from their old creature and metamorphosis has begun to produce the new creature. And, guess what? That Christian crib, warm bottle, and high chair just don't fit anymore! I remember being so intrigued years ago with Psalm 37:4, *"Delight thyself also in the LORD; and he shall give thee the desires of thine heart"* (KJV). I couldn't figure out how to delight myself in Him, which led to this being the very first verse I ever researched in Strong's Concordance. I found that *delight* comes from the Hebrew word `*anag* (Strong's #6026, aw-nag') meaning to be soft or pliable. If you are completely moldable (soft and pliable) in God's hands allowing Him to transform you into a new spiritual creature, of course He can give you the desires of your heart. Wow, all we have to do is become "Gumby" for God!

In the animal world, this transformation occurs naturally as the infant's internal organs begin to disintegrate (liquifying) to be replaced with the adult's internal organs. The disintegration of the infant state is so complete at times, even the outer skin is removed. Scripture tells us that in some cases the Lord removes the outer skin of man's heart or soul: *"The LORD thy God will circumcise thine* heart *(soul), and the heart of thy seed, to love the LORD thy God with all thine heart* (Strong's/Gesenius #3824, also Briggs-Driver-Brown)*, and with all thy soul* (Strong's/Gesenius #5315, also Briggs-Driver-Brown)*, that thou mayest live"* (Deuteronomy 30:6, KJV). The prophet Jeremiah told the people of Israel, *"Circumcise yourselves to the LORD, and take away the foreskins of your heart (#3824), ye men of Judah and inhabitants of Jerusalem: lest my fury come forth like fire, and burn that none can quench it, because of the evil of your doings"* (Jeremiah 4:4, KJV).

The Hebrew word in the original manuscripts translated here as circumcise is *muwl* (Strong's #4135, mool), meaning to cut short, to destroy. The Hebrew word in the original manuscripts translated here as heart is *lebab* (Strong's/Gesenius #3824, lay-bawb'), meaning (in part) the mind, will, appetites, emotions, and courage. The Hebrew word translated here as soul is *nephesh* (Strong's/Gesenius #5315, neh'-fesh), meaning the activity of the character, the soul, of a man.

Whether God does the cutting away of the excess of the heart (soul), or we do it ourselves, I see one advantage to choosing the latter here: cooperating fully with the paring, pruning, cleaning up of our own lives will be much more expedient and less painful than resisting it. I'm quite tired of the pain that my soul's resistance brings when God is always having to "work on" me. I am striving to now "work with" Him instead, and I'm doing it by loosing, stripping, and tearing apart all of my soul's foolish and faulty logic and reasoning for resisting. He is calling you to do the same. You can do it!

I would like to end this chapter by going back to basics and <u>reintroducing you to your first love</u> with this prayer:

Salvation Assurance

I bless you and thank you, Jesus, for what you have done for me. I bind myself to the truth that my salvation has nothing to do with my works. For it was by your grace, your precious favor, that I have been adopted into God's family. My spirit's salvation was never a question of my will or my effort, nor my own willingness to run a race to win it, but it is a gift of your sacrifice and grace. O, Lord, I bind myself to the eternal truth in these words. Help me to ever know that if this great gift was not given to me because of any good thing I did do or any bad thing I did not do, then I cannot lose it by failing to be perfect.

I bind myself to the truth that I have not washed myself, I have not cleaned sin's stain from myself. Rather, by His mercy, God has saved me by the washing and renewing of the Holy Ghost (Titus 3:5,6). I have been found and saved because the Son of Man, God's own Son, came to seek and to save that which was lost. Once I was lost, but now I am found! Yahoo! Thank you, Lord. Even when I was as good as dead in my deepest sin, God's love quickened me to Christ who gave me everlasting life (Ephesians 2:4,5; John 6:47).

I loose all wrong beliefs that it is now up to me to "stay" saved, that I must perform, that I must become perfect through my own efforts. Jesus, help me to realize that as I make more and more room to receive more of you within my soul, I move more and more into my positional standing as a fully free new creature in you. I loose all wrong ideas and beliefs, religious half truths and bondages, and soulish desires to try to win your favor. I bind my will to the will of God, and I choose to surrender to and keep His commandments, obeying His Word, but never from fear because of what I might suffer if I don't. I will keep His commandments because the One I love has loved me more (John 14:21).

Because I love you, I will cause my heart (my soul) to turn away from sin. But if I should sin, you are my advocate with the Father. I will confess my sin and because you are faithful, I will receive forgiveness and cleansing from my unrighteousness (1 John 2:1; 1 John 1:9). If another person has a quarrel against me, I will forgive. I will forgive those whom I have an offense against, just as my Father has forgiven me.

I loose all influences and effects of wrong agreements I have entered into. I have received eternal grace and position with God the Father because of the most important right agreement I have ever entered into, agreeing in full faith that you died for me so I could receive the greatest gift ever given. If you loved me enough to ask your Son to die for me, Father, how could I ever doubt if you love me? I cannot and I will not. Thank you, Lord. Amen.

3

Apple Tree Destiny

Apple Seeds

An apple tree needs no teaching or training whatsoever to realize its destiny to produce apples. Have you ever thought about that? Every tiny apple seed has all of the instructions it ever needs within its own cellular structure to produce sweet fruit, <u>the promise of its destiny</u>. Every seed automatically knows how to become a beautiful, fruit bearing apple tree.

You will never see an apple tree stressing out and feeling pressured over what it should do next. Why not? Because the apple tree knows it is fully supplied with all it needs to produce sweet fruit! Pressure is what we feel when we don't know how we are ever going to get something done. Jesus never showed any stress and pressure during His ministry because He knew His Father's purpose for Him. Nowhere in the Word do we read about Him wringing His hands, crying out, "Hurry up, hurry up, Peter. The wind is coming up and we'll never get across that lake in that little boat if we don't hurry. Andrew, did you bring the bait? Do we have enough nets? When is John going to get here? Who saw John last? What is he doing, doesn't he know how important it is that we stay on time?" No, thank you dear Lord, Jesus never let pressure get to Him. He knew His purpose.

Jesus Christ, implanted within your born again spirit, is the incorruptible Seed of life. His full spiritual structure/stature is within that Seed placed into the born again spirits of all Christians. In Romans 4:16 (AMP), the Apostle Paul speaks of the seed of Abraham: *"Therefore (inheriting) the promise is the outcome of faith and depends (entirely) on faith, in order that it might be given as an act of grace (unmerited favor), to make it stable and valid and guaranteed to all his descendants; not only to the devotees and adherents of the Law but also to those who share the faith of Abraham, who is (thus) the father of us all."* I am so glad that the promise coming to you and me has not had to depend upon every succeeding physical generation of Abraham. God knew better than to trust such a producing of His promise to man's descendants.

This promise was not only to Abraham's physical descendants, *"but also to those who are of the faith of Abraham"* (Romans 4:16). This meant those yet to be born who would imitate Abraham's character, whether they came from his lineage as an Israelite or not. Moses wrote (in Genesis 15:6) of Abraham, as did Paul and James, that **Abraham believed God**. In the Amplified Bible, Galatians 3:6 is translated like this, *"Thus Abraham believed and ahered to and trusted in and* *relied on God, and it was reckoned and placed to his account and accredited as righteousness—as conformity to the divine will in purpose, thought and action."* Wow. That translates for me as righteousness being conformity, agreement, with the will of God in purpose/spirit, thought/soul, and action/body. This has to be a very important point for it was first recorded in Genesis 15:6, then in Romans 4:4, Galatians 3:6, and James 2:23.

If you find it hard to relate to Abraham, the patriarch of Israel, as having anything to do with apple seeds and incorruptible seeds and you, Galatians 3:16 (AMP) should help: *"Now the promises (covenants, agreements) were decreed and made to Abraham and his Seed (his Offspring, his Heir). He (God) does not say, And to seeds (descendants, heirs), as if referring to many persons; but, And to your Seed (your Descendant, your Heir), obviously referring to one individual, Who is (none other than) Christ, the Messiah."*

Every promise made by God to Abraham became "encoded" into the incorruptible Seed of Christ's life which is now in you. I am amazed every time I realize that God chose us to be the soil for planting of the Seed of His promise. Our destiny is to be holy dirt! What happens if you plant a seed into hard, dry, fallow ground? Unless that ground is broken and crushed to softness, that seed will not be able to bring forth its promise. There is nothing wrong with the seed, the problem is in the dirt, the soil.

There is nothing wrong with the Seed that has been implanted into your spirit. If that Seed has not yet fully produced its divine promise within you, there is a problem with the soil of your soul. You have no need of being taught how to produce the promise in the Seed. You do, however, have need of being taught how to loose, release, and let go of everything in your unsurrendered soul that has hardened and encrusted its soil—preventing the germination and growth of the Seed of your promise. That is the purpose of the keys of the Kingdom, the unlocking of all of the rigidity and hardness that your soul has brought into being through its deception that its stronghold walls are protecting you from further pain and disappointment. The toxic waste of bitterness, anger, fear, confusion, and doubt that your soul has been harboring and hiding within these stronghold walls has intensified the soil's pitiful state.

Christ's Seed Parables

Jesus taught seed parables to His followers regarding the seeds of the sower and the dying of a seed to release the life it holds within its own reproductive genes. The sowing of the seeds by the sower is referring to the seeds of the Good News of the Gospel and the different kinds of heart soil (soul soil) it falls upon. Jesus explained (Mark 4:14-20, KJV), *"The sower soweth the word. And these are they by the way side, where the word is sown; but when they have heard, Satan cometh immediately, and taketh away the word that was sown in their hearts. And these are they likewise which are sown on stony ground; who, when they have heard the word, immediately receive it with gladness; and have no root in themselves, and so endure but for a time: afterward, when affliction or persecution ariseth for the word's sake, immediately they are offended. And these are they which are sown among thorns; such as hear the word, and the cares of this world, and the deceitfulness of riches, and the lusts of other things entering in, choke the word, and it becometh unfruitful. And these are they which are sown on good ground; such as hear the word, and receive it, and bring forth fruit, some thirtyfold, some sixty, and some an hundred."* Any seed received into a willing heart, good soil, will burst forth with all of the promise impregnated in the life of Jesus Christ.

The seed that must die before it can bring forth life refers to Christ speaking of His own death in the first level of this principle. The second level refers to the death of the agendas and desires of the unsurrendered soul before it will cooperate with His life growing within us. The Seed of life (implanted in a born again spirit) must grow out through the soul to bear fruit for the world to see and desire. John 12:24-25 (NKJ) tells us that Jesus said, *"Most assuredly, I say to you, unless a grain* (seed) *of wheat falls into the ground and dies, it remains alone; but if it dies, it produces much grain. He who loves his life will lose it, and he who hates his life in this world will keep it for eternal life."* He who loves and protects his own soulish life will lose out on the promises waiting to burst forth from the Seed of Christ's life. He who rejects and crucifies his own soulish desires will see the promises burst forth from the Seed of Christ's life within him.

The soul must die to its own desires, agendas, lists of wrongs and offenses, humans goals, and personal comfort. This is the recognizing and releasing of the self-will which has so long been promoted as the Christians' right to a free will.

No Need To Be Taught How to Bear Fruit

You have had the fully "encoded and programmed"

(using a natural understanding for a spiritual concept) Seed of life and promise implanted in you as a believer. That Seed knows exactly what to do to work the good works of God that have been uniquely preordained and established in heaven for you to do. That Seed knows exactly what to do so you can walk the good paths and find the good life that God has uniquely preordained and established in heaven for you to walk and live (see Ephesians 2:10, AMP). So what has kept you from living in the fullness of the good works, good paths and good life promised to you? Just everything you have held onto within your unsurrendered soul. No big deal, right? Wrong. It is a very big deal if you do not get these principles into your understanding.

Ideally, from infancy, certain things were supposed to be imparted to you by your parents and family members. Love, nurturing, security, mercy, identity (spiritual, social, gender), principles of God's Word, etc. When you lack any of the foundational building blocks of a whole soul, holes occur in your character and personality. You face life with a weakened sense of identity and security, and little strength to handle life's hardest situations. Blaming your parents, others, and God, fixes nothing. It may make your soul feel better temporarily, but it brings you into wrong agreements with humanism. Wrong agreements always open up ways for demonic darkness to increase your feelings of alienation from God. Without any input from the renewing power of God's love and the life of Christ, your character, personality, and soul remain the composite of what you have been given and taught by imperfect human role models.

Most of us, probably all of us, did not receive all the love, nurturing, identity understanding, spiritual training, acceptance, and sense of security we needed during the time our characters were being formed. All of the right building blocks weren't available to us which left holes in the foundation of our souls and personalities. Still, most of us had enough blocks that we were able to go forward in life. Then cruel things that never should have happened to us happened. Those traumas snatched away from us some of the building blocks we had learned to trust. When something comes out of nowhere and smashes part of your life, any sense of security you had in your soul can be ripped out. Your foundation becomes a little shakier than it was before. Your human inability to resolve the question of why these things happened creates even more shaking to the foundation of who you are. More conflict erupts and you struggle with believing that God really is a good and loving God.

Having to compensate for a life that seems like shifting sands at time encourages you to build rigid walls, be suspicious, and doubt. You begin to rationalize that if you cannot trust your own shifting foundation, how can you trust anyone or anything else, either. Babies are not born with any conceptual understanding of security, love, mercy, hope, trust, or identity. Babies have no idea if they are little boys or girls, if they are cute or funny looking, if they are white or black, or if they are taking in impressions of truth or deception. Everything a baby begins to conceptualize is learned from the modeling of other humans. Some babies have really messed up roles models and end up with holes in their characters.

Some people never had good gender role models as they were growing up and their characters were being formed. Their gender identities were never permanently solidified for them in a true and godly way. When these people become overwhelmed by the force of their unmet needs, the enemy is very good at maneuvering people in wrong lifestyles into position around them—people who understand the pressure of their needs. People with missing blocks in their characters' foundation recognize others with like missing blocks. When comfort and encouragement and acceptance can be found no other place, it is inevitable that even a wrong source of comfort will be embraced to stem a flood of despair and loneliness.

Being a Fruit Bearer

Jesus Christ took 12 disciples with holes in their unsurrendered souls—human souls filled with wrong understanding, wrong attitudes, religious bondage, cultural pride, fear, and finite mindsets—and He poured His character, His identity, His life, His understanding, and His healing into them. He restored, reburbished, renewed, regenerated, and reconditioned those poor disciples' souls and they grew into mighty men whose lives turned upside down the whole known world of their day. He is prepared to pour himself into the souls of any who will make room to receive Him. We have not been asked to teach ourselves how to be like Him, we are only asked to let Him express himself through us to a world that has lost hope.

In the Old Testament, the prophet Jeremiah recorded these prophetic words of God (Jeremiah 31:34 KJV), *"And they shall teach no more every man his neighbour, and every man his brother, saying, Know the LORD: <u>for they shall all know me</u>, from the least of them unto the greatest of them, saith the LORD: for I* *will forgive their iniquity, and I will remember their sin no more."* In the New Testament, 1 John 2:27 (KJV) records these words, *"But the <u>anointing which ye have received of him abideth in you</u>, and ye need not that any man teach you: but as the same anointing teacheth you of all things, and is truth, and is no lie, and even as it hath taught you, ye shall abide in him."*

Jeremiah prophesied that there would come a day when the people of God would no longer have to seek instruction on how to be the people of God. John declares in the New Testament that those who believe in Christ have all of the instruction they will ever need on how to be Christians, it actually abides within them. We have received it from Him, the One who lives within our born again spirits—the One who is waiting for room to abide fully within our human souls (mind, will, emotions). When this full release of His life within us can occur, from spirit to soul and outwards, watch out world! Watch out devil! This is the Christian who will begin tracking down every hindrance to his or her destiny and annihilate it.

The fruit that you bear out of the promise within you is for others, it is not for you to clutch to yourself. Unfortunately, we've been taught and we teach other Christians to do things for rewards from God. Give and it will be given back to you. If you'll give, you'll get. This sets up false expectations of what you deserve after you have given. We must learn to be servants and give of whatever resources we have for the sake of obedience to God's will, not for expectations of blessings and rewards.

I once received a letter from an evangelist who told me that God had told him to build a $10,000,000 training center. He said that God had also told him that if I would give $1,000 towards this center, I would get a 100-fold return. I wrote back and told him to send me $10,000 and he would get his $10,000,000 (a 100-fold return). He took me off his mailing list!

Acceptable to God

Paul exhorted the Roman Christians to understand that even though their born again spirits were connected to the Spirit of their Creator, their souls and bodies still needed to be renewed and submitted before they would fulfill God's will and do God's work. We read his exhortation in Romans 12:1-2 (KJV), *"I beseech you therefore, brethren, by the mercies of God, that ye present your bodies a living sacrifice, holy, acceptable unto God, which is your reasonable service. And be not conformed to this world: but be ye transformed by the renewing of your mind, that ye may prove what is that good, and acceptable, and perfect, will of God"* (KJV).

The human body follows the leading of either the soul or the spirit of an individual. Incapable of making any moral, intellectual, or spiritual decision on its own, the body will direct its functions after the soul or the spirit, whichever one seems to be most in control of the belief systems of the individual. Many of today's Christians have unrenewed minds long cluttered with man's preconceived ideas, religious rituals and routines, revisionist "improvements" on the Word, and man's doctrines of spiritual warfare. Filled with this and the personal clutter of their pasts, they wonder why their Christianity seems so hard to walk out in victory over the conventional wisdom and ideas of success according to the world. Romans 12:2 tells us that we are to have our minds renewed so we are not conformed to the thinking of the worldly, carnal thought patterns of the natural mind.

A battle is declared between the thought patterns of the old creature mind and the thought patterns of the new creature mind renewed by Christ and the Word. The battlefield of the mind is where stronghold thinking becomes locked into place. This "locking in" rigidly sets into granite the human logic and reasoning we use to defend what we have chosen to believe. Unfortunately, our old nature's belief systems are composed of the world's perceptions. Our unsurrendered soul says it doesn't matter if those perceptions are right or wrong, helpful or destructive, godly or otherwise—it is our right even as Christians to create our own personal belief systems out of them. The soul will vigorously fight to protect that self-perceived right.

What Kind of Christian Does God Want?

Some have decided that God wants high-profile, high-power Christians to show the devil and the world that no one had better mess with God's people. This gets very close to the warning in Romans 1:21, *"Because that, when they knew God, they glorified him not as God, neither were thankful; but became vain in their imaginations, and their foolish heart was darkened"* (KJV).

Many think that we need more strength from God so we can be bigger and stronger than the devil. We'll never be bigger and stronger in ourselves than the devil, at least not during our lifetimes on earth. We are not the ones who scare the devil here on earth, but it is the heavenly One who wants to send His power through our bodies, souls, and spirits who scares the devil. The devil knows how pitiful we are in our own power, which is exactly why he tries so hard to keep us from coming into agreement with our heavenly Father's plans for our lives. That right agreement with the will of God links us into His power in every situation we face with our Savior, Jesus Christ, Lord over all.

God wants to give us His strength that we will become better servants to encourage and help others. He wants to give us supernatural power for service to others. The anointing He wants to pour out of us is for service to others. Strength, power, and anointing are never for position, attention, or status. They are for service. God does not confirm and act upon whatever we declare and command to be, thereby exhibiting our power Christian status. We have that backwards, just as we so often do when our soul sees some benefit to tweaking the Word of God. God wants us to obey, humbly confirming and acting upon what He has declared to be. The soul wants credit for the strength and the power exhibited—the born again spirit wants to simply serve and then get out of the way of God getting all the glory.

While in one church meeting, I was explaining why God cannot pour out supernatural power through Christians who still have so many stronghold (unsurrendered to Him) areas in their souls. These strongholds almost always protect false humility. Daily, we must crucify the "flesh" of our personal agendas and self-driven souls. Whatever our soul religiously does for God is always a source of affirmation and pride to it. God must keep the unsurrendered soul from appropriating His glory, and He does this by simply restricting His power from the soul's religious acts.

The example that I generally use while teaching this concept is to represent myself as being filled with unmet needs and strongholds, yet laying hands on a blind person who was suddenly healed and could see. I explain that my soul would be so excited over the attention brought by the miracle that it would hardly be able to wait until the next church meeting so it could testify about the miracle it had wrought.

My soul would probably direct my mouth to say something like this, "Last night I laid hands on the eyes of a blind person and his eyes opened up and they were healed. My hands, see, these hands right here. I laid them right on the blind person's eyes. Oh, of course I give God all the glory. But it was my hands that He used!" This example represents someone desperately wanting to be recognized for his or her part in a miracle, even though a small acknowledgment of God is thrown in. So, to keep us from our own folly, God withholds most of His supernatural power and miracles back from our souls until we can genuinely handle that power as if it had nothing to do with us. *He may work miracles for us, but He will hold back any working of miracles through us.*

As I was teaching this, I pointed in the general direction of a woman to use as an example of a blind person. When I did this, everyone in that section of seats started getting a little bit ditzy. I could tell something was going on, but I continued teaching until I realized that the lady I had pointed towards had on very thick glasses, and she seemed to be looking somewhere short of me. I recognized that this woman was probably legally blind. Being gently guided by the Holy Spirit, I stepped down the aisle and laid my hands upon the woman eyes and began to pray for her, saying, "Now here is the way you should pray for someone and then walk away and get out of God's way." I prayed a short prayer, binding every cell in her body to the will and purposes of God that she would fulfill her end times messenger destiny. I loosed all wrong agreements she had ever come into over her sight, and I loosed all diagnoses ever spoken over her that did not line up with God's destiny purposes for her life. I said amen and turned around, walked back to the podium, and began to continue teaching.

The following morning was the Sunday service. When the podium was turned over to me, I began to share a story and as I glanced over the same general area where the woman had been sitting the evening before, I realized everyone in that section was getting ditzy again. The same woman had her face in her hands, rapidly shaking her head from side to side to indicate NO. Everyone was looking so distracted from my story, I walked over to the woman and asked what was going on. Everyone around her kept nudging her to stand up. I reached out, took her hand, and pulled her to her feet. She was quite shy, but finally spoke into the microphone to say that she had been previously declared legally blind, but by the time she went to bed the night before, her eyesight had begun dramatically improving. She could see many things she had never seen before.

I blessed her, everyone applauded God, and I went back to my opening story. The entire situation had obviously been set up by God the previous evening, anointed by God, and pulled off with a miraculous act of God. I did nothing except follow the leading of the

Holy Ghost and then get back to the business of my calling: teaching the people of that church about the keys of the Kingdom and forgetting all else that had happened.

Divinely Led Daniel

Paul said, *"I press on to take hold of that for which Christ Jesus took hold of me. Brothers, I do not consider myself yet to have taken hold of it. But one thing I do: __Forgetting__ what is behind and straining toward what is ahead, I press on toward the goal to win the prize for which God has called me heavenward in Christ Jesus. All of us who are mature should take such a view of things. And if on some point you think differently, that too God will make clear to you"* (Philippians 3:12-15, NIV). The word here translated as forgetting comes from the Greek word *epilanthanomai* (Strong's/Thayers #1950—ep-ee-lan-than'-om-ahee) which means: to lose out of mind; to neglect; to forget; to no longer care for; to give over to oblivion. I call it taking memories and offenses and old beliefs off the life support system that your soul wants to keep them on.

Oh, that we would all consider everything that has ever happened to us—all the circumstances and situations, all of the moments of self-glory, all of the abuses and slights—to be unimportant and remove them from our mind's showroom window. Then we would no longer carefully guard and keep the offenses on life support, or tell again and again of past deeds we'd done. Hopefully we would neglect them completely, depriving our souls of all opportunity to keep them alive!

In Daniel 3:1, King Nebuchadnezzar had an image made of gold, nine feet high and nine feet wide, and he ordered his subjects to bow down to it every time they heard music. If anyone did not bow down immediately, they were to be thrown into a blazing furnace and burned alive. Some astrologers told the king that there were Jews who were not obeying his decree. In verse 13, the king became furious and ordered these Jews brought before him. He commanded Shadrach, Meshach, and Abednego to bow down and worship the golden image, or they would be thrown into the furnace. The young Jewish men replied that they would not, saying, *"If it be so, our God whom we serve is able to deliver us from the burning fiery furnace, and he will deliver us out of thine hand, O king. But if not, be it known unto thee, O king, that we will not serve thy gods, nor worship the golden image which thou hast set up"* (Daniel 3:16-17, KJV).

Nebuchadnezzar had them thrown into a furnace heated seven times hotter than usual. When he looked into the furnace, he saw that there appeared to be four men walking about unharmed in the flames, the fourth one appearing to be like the Son of God (vs. 25). He called to Shadrach, Meschach, and Abednego to come out of the furnace, and they walked out unharmed. At that point in Daniel 3:27-28, we read that *"the satraps, prefects, governors and royal advisers crowded around them. They saw that the fire had not harmed their bodies, nor was a hair of their heads singed; their robes were not scorched, and there was no smell of fire on them. Then Nebuchadnezzar said, 'Praise be to the God of Shadrach, Meshach and Abednego, who has sent his angel and rescued his servants! They trusted in him and defied the king's command and were willing to give up their lives rather than serve or worship any god except their own God'"* (NIV).

70

Most Christians are familiar with this story, a story that can give great hope of what God can do, yet can cause an unsurrendered soul to fear what God might ask His people to go through. All human beings will go through trials and tribulations during their lives, some tragic, some frustrating, some frightening. The human soul reacts to these experiences in varying ways. Many people who have survived a fiery trial never quit talking about it, relating every new day of their lives to the fiery experience they previously went through. They see every new circumstance through the filter of their experience in the fiery trial. They react to new situations, new people, and new challenges out of the accumulation of ashes and smoke and open wounds of their former experience. They smell like smoke!! The fire becomes their point of reference for the rest of their lives.

Others go through the fire of life's experiences like Shadrach, Meschach, and Abednego to come out with no wounds, no burns, no singed hair, no scorched robes, and no smell of fire upon them. What makes the difference? Why do some never see the potential of life after a fiery trial, but remain as if they were still walking in the fire, still breathing the smoke? Why do others walk out of fiery trials, acknowledging that it may not have been pleasant, but they will grow from the experience and become stronger for it. They never look back and there is no smell of the smoke upon them. Some people become so involved in their grieving about the experience, it is almost as if they become addicted to the grief. Here is a prayer to bring the soul to a place of surrendering its grief:

Grief

Jesus, I have lost someone (or something) very dear to me. I feel such pain and grief in my soul right now. I also feel overwhelming anger, confusion, and fear. Anger because my loss is not fair. Confusion because I do not understand why it has happened. Fear because I don't know what else I might lose. You have said that all things work together for good for those who know and love you, but I do not know what possible good lies in this loss. But I must trust you to work it to good. Help me to surrender my questions and this unresolved issue to you and make room to receive your grace and comfort. I need to make room in my pain and grief for your joy, peace, and comfort.

My heart hurts, and I need your love and strength. Your Word says that my heart is my mind, will, and emotions. So, I bind my mind, my will, and my emotions to your will and purposes for my life right now. I need and I choose to embrace Christ's assurance in my mind that I will know joy, peace, and hope again. I need and I choose to hold tight to your will for me as my life moves beyond this loss. I need and I choose your healing grace and mercy for my emotions. I bind myself to the truth that you will comfort and heal me, that you have plans and purposes for me beyond this time, and they are for good.

I will not insist upon a question mark where you have placed a period. You have not asked me to bury my feelings of grief, but I will use them as an open door to press closer to you. I bind my mind to the mind of Christ and loose wrong thought patterns. I loose all thoughts of "if only I had . . . what if I had . . . why didn't I. . . . " I loose denial and hopelessness from my soul. I loose all soul ties to my lost (person, opportunity, thing), and I choose to let go, knowing overcoming and healing will not mean I have forgotten a loved one. I bind my mind to the truth that overcoming and healing through your strength means I will be able to freely think on the good memories I have without fearing an encounter with unresolved pain. I will not grieve over what could have been, rather I bind myself—body, soul, and spirit—to your good plans from this point forward in my life.

After King David's infant son died, he said, "I shall go to him, but he will not return to me." Lord, help me to recognize that if I have lost a loved one who believed in Christ, I will see that one again. If my loved one had not professed belief in Christ as far as I knew, I do not know what his/her final words with the Holy Spirit were before he/she died. But I can know the blessing of hope that my prayers while he/she was alive opened up a final few perfect moments for such a talk. You are my strength and my source, you are my comforter and my guide. I will trust and follow you out of this valley of sadness. Bless the Lord, O my soul. For Jesus is my everything.

Consequences: Natural or Spiritual?

No matter how seriously you attempt to practice self-discipline on your unsurrendered soul to make it acceptable to Jesus Christ, consequences will just keep boiling up around you. Your finite thinking processes are incapable of determining perfect choices. Even slightly imperfect choices produce slightly wrong consequences that can quickly grow into hugely wrong ones when they are left to their own resolution. Your self-discipline will always just be a temporary, front line measure that needs to be constantly reinforced and policed by your will. It will never be a settled, done issue. God will expose your best attempts to act out that which is not a spiritual reality in your soul.

"But, I try so hard!" you may wail. You will have to keep trying harder and harder as long as your soul is not surrendered to the reality that God wants in you. God wants you to surrender your total being to Him so that you draw upon His power and love to be a life-filled, life-giving, life-loving Christian. Such a state of living can be a settled thing. Just know this for a fact: God won't be a traffic cop to keep your "free will" out of dire trouble if you insist upon living your life your way. Your way will always produce consequences that must be walked out in the natural realm of life—consequences that have nothing to do with what God wants for you to walk out in the spiritual realm of life. When you don't understand, believe in, or know how to receive God's grace to walk in truth, you must constantly reinforce your own own self-protection and self-defense systems. His healing grace can't flow into your deepest pain and need if you don't know how to make your soul release its safeguard systems.

Hard biting consequences are the illegitimate children of wrong choices. As Christians we are to judge ourselves, not to try to justify ourselves. If you don't judge yourself, God will judge you, and He will chastise. If you try to justify yourself, God won't justify you, and the chastisement may be heavier. Repenting to God of your wrong choices will get you forgiven, but it may not eliminate the consequences. Rationalizing and justifying your wrong choices to God will produce even more consequences, consequences that can end up being driven by forces of darkness as well.

The only human I know of who walked this earth with body, soul, and spirit in perfect alignment with God's will rather than His own will, walked on water, raised the dead, touched blind eyes and had them open. Everything He touched in the natural had spiritual consequences. He said, *"Now I'm going back to the Father to prepare a place for you up there."* That place is where you are going to live when your life goes into phase two: eternity. What you learn here is what you are going to take into eternity with you. God will see that you learn what you need to before you enter eternity (even it you think it is going to kill you while you are still here learning it—it won't).

You can be a college professor, a grandma sitting at home knitting lap robes, a dishwasher, or a computer data entry operator—God will use whatever is around you and in your life to see that you are adequately trained for your destiny. He doesn't care where you're working or not working, He's going to bring forth life and the promise producing principles you need and <u>you will learn them somehow</u>!

Encouraging Yourself In the Lord

Thank you, Lord, for recording in your Word that you did not turn Thomas away from you when he struggled with doubt. Nor did you turn Peter away when he struggled with fear of being aligned with knowing you. I'm struggling and I'm fearful now, and I come to you for encouragement, strength, and assurance. I bind myself to your truth with all its

promises, blessings, hope, faith, and covenants. I loose
all of my worries and anxieties over what has happened
before and what will happen next

I thank you for this moment of rest in the present
tense of your love today. Right now, the past is gone
and the present is not yet, and I bind myself to your
timing for all things. I loose all thought patterns and
old mindsets that cause me to be preoccupied with either
the past or the present, and I will enjoy this present
time with you. You are my present-tense God. I bind
my mind to the mind of Christ, needing and expecting
an infilling of His thoughts and peace. I loose all wrong
patterns of thinking, wrong beliefs, wrong ideas, wrong
mindsets, and wrong agendas of my soul. I loose all
fear from my emotions, determining to address every
human and demonic attack on my peace first and always
with the keys of the Kingdom prayer principles. I will
first realign myself with you, and then I will address
the attack.

O, Father God, your Word promises me that it is
your **good pleasure** to give me the Kingdom (Luke 12:
32); it is your **good pleasure** to adopt me as your own
(Ephesians 1:5); it is your **good pleasure** to see that I
know the mystery of your will (Ephesians 1:9); that
you are working in me to will and to do your **good
pleasure** (Philippians 2:13); and that you will fulfill
all of the **good pleasure** of your goodness that Christ
would be glorified in me and I in Him (2 Thessalonians
1:11-12). O, Lord, your Word promises me that my
eyes, ears, and heart don't have a clue yet of the good
things you have prepared for me (Isaiah 64:4; 1
Corinthians 2:9). I bind my mind, will, and emotions
to these truths for my own good pleasure. I will rejoice
in your promises. Your Word says that you will preserve

me from evil, you will preserve my soul, you will preserve my going out and my coming in, now and forever (Psalms 121:7-8). Your Word says that you are with me, I am not to fear or be dismayed, for you are my God and you will help me (Isaiah 41:10). Your Word says that I can peacefully lie down in sweet sleep wherever you have put me, for you see that I dwell in safety (Psalms 4:8; Proverbs 3:24).

I bind my mind, will, and emotions to these truths of your protection. I bind my will to your will and my feet to the paths you want me to walk that I will be where you want me to be. I will rejoice in your promises. Bless the Lord, O my soul, and forget not His love, His benefits, and His grace. Amen.

4

Fine Tuning Your
Kingdom Principles

Praying Right Prayers

Second Chronicles 7:14 (KJV) tells us that God has said, *"If my people, which are called by my name, shall humble themselves, and pray, and seek my face, and turn from their wicked ways; then will I hear from heaven, and will forgive their sin, and will heal their land."* The keys of the Kingdom principles of binding and loosing prayers give you what you need: 1) To humble your own soul and bring it into alignment with the prayers your spirit knows it needs to pray, 2) to loose the distractions of your soul and the world that keep you from seeking His face, and 3) to cut your soul's attempts to stop you from loosing its carnal and wicked agendas.

This is pretty straight forward stuff which allows no denial, no excuses, no rationalizing, no justifying. No blame shifting, no hunting for who started it, no hunting for who is working the hardest to continue it. Just a direct statement from God as to how to get it resolved. I love how Peterson translates John 9:1-3 in *The Message: "Walking down the street, Jesus saw a man blind from birth. His disciples asked, 'Rabbi, who sinned: this man or his parents, causing him to be born blind?' Jesus said, 'You're asking the wrong question. You're looking for someone to blame. There is no such cause-effect here. Look instead for what God can do.'"*

If we cooperate with Him, if we focus on working with Him to see what He can do instead of trying to look for someone to blame, just what might God do in us and through us? One thing Jesus said He would do is make us fountains of living waters: *"Whoever drinks of the water that I shall give him will never thirst. But the water that I shall give him will become in him a fountain of water springing up into everlasting life"* (John 4:14, NKJ). Is that fountain or river of life gushing forth from within you right now? Or are you a human example of drip irrigation wherever you go? Maybe just one big drip? (Sorry, I couldn't help myself.)

Well, there is certainly nothing wrong with the source of the river, is there? So your river bed must be clogged up. Your soul will allow you to consider that. It will even appear to work with you on clearing out some of the clogs that its tenacious record-keeping system has established—if you work at clearing them with a teaspoon (perhaps a tablespoon if you really push it). The keys of the Kingdom, binding and loosing, go after those clogs with a spiritual backhoe. So, just how fast do you want to clear out the old "stuff" your soul has carefully preserved and is now pretending to help you remove?

If your soul can keep you picking away spoonful by spoonful at all of your old stuff, it can agree with or fight against every little thing you're trying to spoon out. However, if you go at the clogs in your soul with a spiritual backhoe, you will get a big time reaction from your soul—yes, indeed, you will. It will start screaming, "No, no, you can't throw all of that out at once. I don't know what's in there. I haven't been able to examine it piece by piece to see if there is something I want to hold onto." Well, duh! That's the whole idea, soul.

God's grace covers a lot of our soulish carnal mistakes while we're caught in the heat of the conflict between our souls and spirits. But God's full river of blessing and empowerment cannot come until we're willing to choose to let go of the crud of that conflict.

Binding and Loosing Is Better

When I first began to pray with the keys of the Kingdom, I believed I heard God say to bind my will to His will. God said to me that the binding key was like a safety harness, a seat belt attached to Him. Although it is commonly understood in Christianity that our own unsurrendered will can be quite hard to deal with as a new believer, there are not very many actual references to man's will in the Scriptures. The word "heart" is used instead, referring to an ever-shifting collaboration of the different entities of the human mind, will, and emotions (more on this later in the chapter). So, I began to bind my will to the will of God, my mind to the mind

81

of Christ, my emotions to the balance and control of the Holy Ghost, and essentially "all" three to the truth of His Word. I was putting on my spiritual seat belt.

Matthew 16:19 and Matthew 18:18 clearly tell us that Jesus said, *"Whatsoever you bind/loose on earth will be bound/loosed in heaven."* The Hebrew and Greek words for "bind" and "binding" mean some very positive things—to hold, undergird, heal, knit, put under obligation, fasten, tie, weave together, wind around, and cause fragmented pieces to coalesce and become one again—amongst other things (see *Shattering Your Strongholds* for further word studies).

Paul said (Acts 20:22, KJV), *"And now, behold, I go bound* (Greek: compelled by his convictions to follow through on what he had determined the Lord's will was) *in the spirit* (Greek: the power by which a human being feels, thinks, wills, decides, i.e. the soul) *unto Jerusalem, not knowing the things that shall befall me there."* This is a powerful translation of Paul's feeling compelled in his soul to do the Lord's will. Paul had evidently so determined that his soul would cooperate in the producing of the promise that Christ had imbedded within him, that it did without so much as a peep.

Paul also said, *"I am persuaded, that neither death, nor life, nor angels, nor principalities, nor powers, nor things present, nor things to come, nor height, nor depth, nor any other creature, shall be able to separate us from the love of God, which is in Christ Jesus our Lord"* (Romans 8:38-39, KJV). He uses this same word again in, *"For the which cause I also suffer these things: nevertheless I am not ashamed: for I know whom I have believed, and am persuaded that he is able to keep that which I have committed unto him against that day"* (2 Timothy 1:12, KJV).

The Greek word translated as persuaded in both of these verses is Strong's #3982 *peitho,* pi'-tho, (initially described in Thayers #3982 as "to bind") meaning to be induced to believe, to have faith. I am not fully certain of the correlation between these two meanings, but I do believe that "to bind one's self" could be related to inducing one's self to believe and have faith that Christ is able to keep us safe from ourselves and everything else as well!

Strong's/Gesenius #6960 tells us that the Hebrew word translated "wait" in Isaiah 40:31, *"But they that wait upon the LORD shall renew their strength; they shall mount up with wings as eagles; they shall run, and not be weary; and they shall walk, and not faint"* (Isaiah 40:31, KJV), is *qavah* (kaw-vaw'). This Hebrew word means to bind together; to gather together; and to expect. What a wonderful concept we could figuratively draw from these definitions: that by binding ourselves collectively to God and His will and purposes (having gathered together), we could corporately expect to rise above our circumstances and renew our strength to run without getting weary.

Don't Let The Put Ons Put You Off

The "put ons" (as well as the "put offs") of the Word of God are quite interesting. Ephesians 4:24 tells us to " . . . *put on the new man, which after God is created in righteousness and true holiness."* Colossians 3:10 tells us to " . . . *put on the new man, which is renewed in knowledge after the image of him that created him."* These words, *put on,* mean to wrap one's self in something as if it were a garment. While this is not stated to mean to bind a garment upon yourself in the original Greek, I feel there is a connection. However, I think Romans 13:14 really gets exciting, as the *put ye on* in this verse (seen after this sentence) means to become so possessed of the mind of Chist in thought, feelings, and actions as to resemble Him, and, as it were, to then reproduce the life He lived (Thayers). Yee-haw! *"Put ye on the Lord Jesus Christ, and make not provision for the flesh, to fulfil the lusts thereof"* (KJV). This makes so much sense in why we should bind our minds to the mind of Christ, whose mind we should have in us according to Scripture (Philippians 2:5).

Ephesians 6:11-18 tells you that you are to: *"Put on the whole armor of God . . . take up the whole armor of God . . . and having done all . . . stand therefore, having girded your waist with truth, having put on the breastplate of righteousness, and having shod your feet with the preparation of the gospel of peace; above all, taking the shield of faith with which you will be able to quench all the fiery darts of the wicked one. And take the helmet of salvation, and the sword of the Spirit, which is the word of God; praying always with all prayer and supplication in the Spirit, being watchful to this end with all perseverance and supplication for all the saints"* (NKJ).

In the listing of the spiritual weapons of Ephesians 6, we find that verse 14 (KJV) says to *"stand therefore, having your loins girt about with truth."* First Peter 1:13 says to *"gird up the loins of your mind, be sober, and hope to the end for the grace that is to be brought unto you at the revelation of Jesus Christ"* (KJV). The Greek word used for girt or gird here, is *anazonnumi* (Strong's/Thayers #328—an-ad-zone'-noo-mee); which metaphorically meant to be prepared, derived from the practice of the Orientals who, in order to be unimpeded in their movements, would bind their long flowing garments closely around their bodies and fasten them with a leather belt to be enencumbered when traveling or working.

You do not put on the "pieces" of the above armor by reciting this list and claiming it for yourself. You prepare or gird yourself by knowing truth, having read it and studied it and used it. You use truth to get on with where you must go and what you must do for your Lord.

You study the Word to to recognize that you haven't done anything to earn righteousness in Him, so you can't lose it. You accept your state as a former sinner who has embraced Christ as your Savior and is now seen as covered with His perfection.

You put on Gospel shoes by preparing yourself through study and prayer to understand how to impart peace and the Good News everywhere you go, remembering that you can't give what you don't have.

You understand that faith is trust and confidence in the goodness of God. If you don't have perfect trust in what He may do, you research declarations of His goodness in the Word. Your knowledge of His trustworthiness and goodness becomes your shield against lies of the enemy.

You wear your helmet of salvation by bringing the thought patterns and attitudes of your mind into alignment with the promises in the Word about your sure salvation through Christ your Savior.

You constantly renew your understanding (through study and meditation on the Scriptures) of the power of the Word to work both inwardly in your life and outwardly from your life like a two-edged sword. A two-edged sword cuts away from you as well as into you. And having done all this, you pray always.

The Warfare Key of Loosing

According to the original Greek words used for *loose* and its root words *(luo, hragnumi,* and *agnumi),* the loosing key allows me to break up, destroy, dissolve, unloose, melt, put off, wreck, crack to sunder by separation of the parts, shatter into minute fragments, disrupt, lacerate, convulse with spasms, break forth, burst, rend, and tear apart the strongholds of my own mind (see *Shattering Your Strongholds* for further word studies). Yahoo! The Kingdom key of loosing is my key of breaking up, out, and through, to wreak spiritual terrorism on evil spirits. It is my key to perform radical self-surgery on any unsurrendered area in my soul. Loosing is the key that can blow away every stronghold, vain imagination, and high thing (2 Corinthians 10:4-5) that tries to exalt itself between believers and a full knowledge of their loving God and His ways!

According to Thayers Greek/English Lexicon, the Greek word for strongholds as used in 2 Corinthian 10:4-5 (KJV), *"The weapons of our warfare are not carnal, but mighty through God to the pulling down of* strong holds; *casting down imaginations, and every high thing that exalteth itself against the knowledge of God, and bringing into captivity every thought to the obedience of Christ,"* is *ochuroma* (Strong's/Thayers #3794, okh-oo'-ro-mah). This word means the arguments and reasonings an individual uses to fortify his opinions and beliefs and defend them against any opposing viewpoints.

Consider these wrong reasonings, "I couldn't possibly forgive him, because what he did to me was evil and terribly wrong. His cruelty and betrayal has impacted my life so much, he robbed me of my destiny." "She stole the only man I ever loved, so I have never married and had children and it's all her fault." "I'm old and all alone, because of what my family did to me." These are actual statements made to me by hurting people who have no idea that they have built their own strongholds from wrong agreements that every hurt and pain was forever. These people have reasoned themselves into their own dungeons of pain and fear.

Ephesians 4:22 tells us to *put off* the old man and all of his soulish reasoning, taken from Strong's/Thayers #659, *apotithem,* ap-ot-eeth'-ay-mee, meaning to cast off, lay apart, and put away the old man. Colossians 3:8-9 tells us to " . . . *put off all these; anger, wrath, malice, blasphemy, filthy communication out of your mouth. Lie not one to another, seeing that ye have put off the old man with his deeds.* " This translation to *put off* in Colossian 3:8 is the same as above in Ephesians 4:22, while the Colossians 3:9 use of *put off* from *apekduomai* (Strong's/Thayers #554, ap-ek-doo'-om-ahee) means to separate and spoil what is put off. Serious stuff here!

The Anger Needs to Go

How do we put away the anger from violent abuse to ourselves or even harder, violent abuse to one of our loved ones, perhaps our child? That kind of deep seated anger and wrath easily morphs itself into malice directed towards the abuser. Any act of clinging to painful rage in the soul, or an act of retribution in the natural, will never undo what has been done. Only divine power being allowed to enter the soul through using the spiritual key of loosing can separate that kind of negative emotion and bring healing.

In my early days of Christianity, when I was very angry at someone who had hurt me deeply, I remember being told that I had to forgive everyone, every time, all the time regardless of what they had done in my life. I recoiled from that, crying out, "God, that's not fair!"

I remember having a distinct impression that God replied, *"I don't deal in fair. I deal in what is right and what is best for all involved."* I struggled with complying with this command of God's Word (see chapter on forgiveness in *Shattering Your Strongholds*). It wasn't until years later when I began to understand the power of binding my will to the will of God and loosing all of the rigid mindsets and old patterns of thinking toward those who had hurt me, that I began to receive empowerment from the Lord to enable me to forgive freely. Forgiveness does not set the one who inflicts the hurt free, it frees the one who has been reliving the pain and traumatic memories over and over in his or her mind. Forgiveness is not proof of super sainthood, forgiveness is God's "get out of your soul's jail free" card so you can get on with your life's destiny—the good works, the good paths, the good life (Ephesians 2:10, AMP). The details of how He deals with the other people are none of our business. We're freed from the pain and pushed towards the future He wants us to fulfill.

I have spent time with some people who have faithfully pressed into these principles and used the binding and loosing prayers on their own souls for years. They have seen many breakthroughs, yet some still quite can't quite seem to get that final freedom to plunge into the "bigger than life" Christian experience God created them to live. Some Christians just keep methodically breaking through, loosing each wall their poor, frantic little souls keep throwing up. Sometimes, they are actually loosing air as nothing is there. Still, they are like urgent little Energizer™ Bunnies who just keep going and going and going, no matter what gets in their way—or what they think is in their way. They just need some "fine tuning" on their binding and loosing skills.

Fine Tuning Your Binding and Loosing Skills

The following paragraphs may need a warning label for those who are not yet into this whole "dying to self" thing. If you are not yet even praying the binding and loosing basics for yourself, you may choke up before you're through reading this. These words won't be fatal to your future, however much your unsurrendered soul fears their potential for carving up its hold on you.

The basic binding principles begin with binding your will to the will of God. This unfortunately is not a once and for all thing. It requires repeated efforts on your part to keep your will at the foot of the Cross, for it keeps trying to sneakily crawl away every chance it gets. Every confrontation with our wills should be viewed as another obedience class session for the chronically willful.

Ephesians 2:10 (AMP) says, *"We are God's own handiwork (His workmanship) recreated in Christ Jesus, (born anew) that we may do those good works which God predestined (planned beforehand) for us, (taking paths which He prepared ahead of time) that we should walk in them—living the good life which He prearranged and made ready for us to live."* I used to be very queasy about the word "predestination," not wanting to believe that I had little or no choice in anything of my life, Christian or otherwise. I had very narrow thinking regarding choices—either they were all mine or none of them were. It never occurred to me in my early days with God that His choices for me might be better and more exciting than the precious right to my free will's choices that I was so desperately clinging to.

Predestination is not a life of being controlled by God. We are all allowed our own choices, repeatedly. A right choice (one that agrees with His plans for us) will always lead us into the good works, the good paths, the good life that He has purposed for us to enjoy. A wrong choice will always lead us away from our preordained destiny as overcomers, saints, and winners. I am reminded of those "multiple-choice endings" young peoples' books of years gone by. As you read, you would find yourself facing a "choice" which might read something like this: "If you want to choose to go back into the barn, turn to page 19 and continue reading. If you want to choose to get on the bus, turn to page 27 and continue reading." In effect, you controlled the story's outcome by the choices you made. Most of these books attempted to show young people that all choices have consequences. Right choices create good consequences, wrong choices create difficult consequences. Some of the books showed that making wrong choices kept bringing you back to those same choices over and over, like a rat in a rigged maze.

Set Your Stakes

We must choose to believe that God's Word is true

and forever. We must bind ourselves to this truth, driving it into our souls like a stake that can never be pulled up. Only then will some of us have the courage to believe that we will actually see our lives become the promise Jesus Christ wants to produce through us. Paul said in Colossians 3:15-16 (AMP) that you should *"let the peace of God rule in your hearts, to which also you were called in one body; and be thankful. Let the word of Christ dwell in you richly in all wisdom, teaching and admonishing one another in psalms and hymns and spiritual songs, singing with grace in your hearts to the Lord"* (NKJ).

We have done nothing to be able to produce anything of eternal value, except for one glorious moment of eternal right behavior when we chose to accept Jesus Christ as our Lord and Savior—the most important choice we have ever made. The Apostle Paul encourages me with these words that I indeed did drive down a stake in my life with that act: *"Although you at one time were estranged and alienated from Him and of hostile attitude of mind in your wicked activities, yet now has (Christ, the Messiah,) reconciled (you to God) in the body of His flesh through death, in order to present you holy and faultless and irreproachable in His (the Father's) presence"* (Colossians 1:21-22, AMP). Jesus Christ did the hard part, now all I have to do is believe it and stay settled in it. I can do this! It is not our works, our behaviors, our agendas, but it is what Christ did for us that makes us acceptable to the Father. That will never change.

Many have an understanding of persistent prayer as meaning that eventually we will change God's mind to do something for us that He doesn't really want to do. The example of the persistent widow with the unjust judge (Luke 18:6) has long been used to back up this erroneous belief. God is not an unjust judge, so how can we equate the unjust judge's role here with the role of our Heavenly Father? Would this story perhaps be more applicable to our insisting that the world do what is right?

Consider the times God has not seemed to answer your prayers—perfectly good prayers asking for perfectly good things (in your eyes). God doesn't answer our very "best" prayers at times because what we've asked for would enable us to stay rooted right where we are in mediocrity, or enable us to hold onto something we do not want to release, or enable us to head down a path away from where He wants us to go. God does not even always respond to prayers of seeming great need, when the soul is in control. He does always respond, however, to obedience and surrender, when the soul is no longer controlling a life. I have heard God say, *"If you want to get everything you pray for, just pray right prayers."* Prayers for His will to be done.

Understanding: Self-Perception or Reality?

While researching some words in the original Greek of the New Testament, I looked up the words "understand/understanding" in several different resources. To truly understand something means to bring your perception of a thing or a circumstance into alignment with the reality of it. We humans are very prone to want to try to force a mental alteration of the reality of something into a perception that our mind finds it easier to deal with. So, we often allow our mind to get very creative with our memories and perceptions of things out of our pasts, things that have never been resolved for us. Altering our perception of reality is always involved in fantasizing.

Fantasizing is an interesting subject, although a little dangerous to the healing and wholeness of the soul. I have been studying endorphins from a layman's point of view for some time now. It is not yet easy to find any endorphin studies that the average non-medical person can readily absorb—so please know I am aware of having a fairly superficial knowledge here. Endorphins seem to be a feel good hormone the body will produce in response to certain activities. I have read that there are receptor sites in your brain that receive these hormones and inform the rest of you that you feel really good. If your life gets put together fairly well as a child, you would probably learn to experience the release of these hormones through intellectual activity, creative activity, physical exercise, and pleasurable activities with people you enjoy. Sexual activity, which should be learned in marriage, also releases these hormones.

There are fairly recent studies showing that men who are addicted to pornography actually have something similar to pathways etched into their brains that endorphins travel over when released by viewing sexual imagery. I had believed that pornography addiction and sexual addiction was a matter of the soul's unmet needs sending out drives that were interpreted as sexual needs. It appears, however, that sexual addiction is not only a mental and an emotional reaction to unmet needs. These studies suggest that these brain pathways used by endorphin releases stimulated by pornography create a physiological addiction as well.

When a child learns to expect the release of endorphins from inappropriate activities, such as early sexual activity or sexual abuse, this can become a big problem later on in life.

In the early part of 1999, there was a truly frightening trend of kids killing other kids as well as teachers, even their own parents. In reading a newspaper editorial recently, I was intrigued with one teenager's comment on these killings. The letter referred to the fantasies that teenage boys live out in violent video games and movies, becoming so immersed in the excitement of hunting and killing and revenge that they lose touch with what is not reality and what is. I also gathered from the studies of endorphins that there seems to be a gradual decrease in the endorphin hormone's ability to produce the same level of exciting feelings. So the stimulus has to be increased to release a larger quantity.

It does not seem irrational to believe that when violent video games and movies cease to provide adequate hormonal endorphin releases to reach the internal high previously reached, that a next step would be sought. The next step to up the stimulus could easily be to seek such thrills in the real world, a rather paradoxical expression to use here as it seems the teenage boys involved in these killings are totally out of touch with the real world that most people recognize.

Altered Reality

Many people who have been deeply hurt, yet are in denial of still being in bondage to that unhealed hurt, will insist that they appreciate and can handle truth. They will look you right in the eye and urge you to tell

94

them what you honestly think about situations in their lives. I think they sincerely believe what they say, but when you tell them straight up truth—they are angered or devastated by it. Why? The truth is totally out of alignment with their perceptions of themselves. They perceive themselves as being strong and open and transparent (what they believe they are), while they are wounded and bleeding in their souls.

Hidden behind their denial of their souls' inner fragility is this truth: "I can receive any form of information that will line up with the altered reality that my soul has determined about this issue." The problem here is that their altered perception of reality is a deception that has been exquisitely reprocessed into something they can deal with. Any truth from another human being can be painfully jarring to that fragile structure of misunderstanding. The really bad part of this coping mechanism is that generally they are the only ones who are deceived. Other people, with devious agendas, are quite capable of devising ways of manipulating this person through their deceptions. Satan is quite aware of the deception and knows how to bring people around this person who are able to push all of the right buttons and raw spots to produce ricochet reactions that send the person in exactly the direction he desires.

If you are really good at this mental game, how do other people know that you're not who you perceive and project yourself to be? Some people will be fooled, particularly people who are deliberately moving within the most shallow depths of reality themselves. Even this choice, to see everything at surface value, is a coping mechanism. Shallow can be easily dismissed if it doesn't line up with your perception of yourself and the world around you. Shallow waters can be your friend if you can't handle reality's deeper waters. But there are many people who see through these facades and when they have hidden agendas, they usually know how to use and manipulate the deceived person to meet their own agendas.

Reality exists, and it is always waiting to jump out and confront you when you least expect it. Learning to see things as God sees them can take a lot of pressure off the one trying so hard to maintain an altered perception of life. Altered reality is ever shifting, requiring constant maintenance of the smoke screens, the soft fuzzy clouds, the cracked mirrors. Real truth is a constant that maintains its own integrity.

True Sacrifice Is Voluntary

There is a difference between sacrificing something and having something taken from you. True sacrifice is always voluntary. Having something taken from you is a loss, perhaps even a violation.

As I was ministering to someone one time, I said, "You are so frightened about finances. As much as you love the Lord, your bottom-line sense of security really is attached to money, isn't it? God may require you to make a financial sacrifice to Him to prove to yourself that He will take care of you. Why don't you give a real sacrificial offering to that little mission downtown?"

Her instant response was, "I have already sacrificed my business to Him. I thought that was enough. Shouldn't that satisfy Him?"

I realized that she had a wrong belief about why she had lost her business, and had rationalized it as a sacrifice to God. She had felt financially secure because she had experienced income for nearly two years that she believed she controlled. When the business failed, she had rationalized that loss as a sacrifice that God had demanded of her. And somewhere in her mind, she felt God owed her a payback. She wasn't going to give Him any more until He fulfilled His obligation to her. This was quite a deception, and it was holding her in financial bondage. It was also dangerously close to accusing God of reneging on His responsibilities.

I said, "Joy, you didn't sacrifice your business to God. You lost your business because you didn't handle your finances wisely—that was wrong finite thinking and lack of budgeting and planning on your part. The business represented a form of security to you that you were not willing to trust God with, an area that you wanted Him to keep His hands away from. Without His intervention and His guidance, you couldn't keep the business going on your own. The natural economic principles of business that you didn't know how to make work for you caused you to lose your business. God did not ask you or make you sacrifice it to Him." Sacrifice is always a voluntary giving of something.

Financial Provision Assurance

Lord, your Word says that if I seek first your Kingdom and Christ's righteousness, then all things will be added unto me (Matthew 6:33). Your Word says that if I will forsake all for your Kingdom's sake, then I shall receive back more than I have forsaken in this age as well as in the ages yet to come. If all things have not yet been added unto me (and they haven't), then I have not truly put your Kingdom and Christ's righteousness completely first. Lord, I bind myself to your truth. Please show me errors in my thinking so I don't deceive myself over this.

I have often felt I have sacrificed so much for you. Lord, help me to understand what sacrifice means. It is not having to surrender something because I have no choice. It is not having to let go of something because it is a law of the land. It is not to have something taken from me. Sacrifice means to voluntarily give up something for the sake of a more pressing claim—that being your will and your desire for my life. My true sacrifice must be to surrender my trust in that which I believe gives me security and control over most of the situations I might face—money. I admit that I have not really sacrificed as much as I would like to think.

Jesus said that the poor in spirit were blessed. Help me to understand that the word "spirit" here means my soul—my mind, will, and emotions. Help me to understand that the word poor used here means to voluntarily choose to make my soul poor, to surrender my will. Lord, I now choose to loose, sever, cut, dissolve, and put off all self-motivated desires, all self- perceived need, all self- drives coming out of my unmet needs that cause me to worry that I am not going to have enough money. Dear Jesus, I want to stop worrying about money. Worry is just a substitute for prayer and faith in your goodness and promised provision.

Regardless of all the prosperity Scriptures I have learned to quote, you are under no obligation to provide funding and resources so I can pursue my will, or so I can pursue what I have decided must be your will. But you have promised that you will always provide for those who are walking as fully as they know how in order to see that your will would be done in their own sphere of influence and in all of the earth.

Lord, you say in Isaiah (58:7) that we are to share our food with the hungry, we are to provide the poor wanderer with shelter, we are to clothe the naked when we see them, and we are not to turn away from our own flesh and blood in their needs of any kind. We are not called to judge how people came upon hard times, but we are to give out of whatever we have to help alleviate their suffering. I believe you will provide all I need as I pursue your will as purely as I know how. Amen.

Souls? Spirits? Does it Really Matter?

It is very important for a Christian to understand the difference between the human soul and the human spirit, as well as to recognize the workings of the unsurrendered human soul versus manifestations of evil spirits. These can be confusing differences to determine from a finite point of view. Today's Christians need a much deeper understanding of why we, the body of Christ, have continually seemed to spin our wheels with our spiritual warfare tactics—always fighting for every inch of ground we take from the forces of darkness. Then we continue having to fight to try to hold onto it. With the enormous outpouring of the Good News of the Gospel of Jesus Christ from so many sources today, i.e. satellite television, cable television programs, radio programs, tapes, videos, conferences, books, and more, wouldn't you think that the Church should be having a much higher ratio of success than it does?

Haven't we all wondered why overcoming and spiritual victory can seem to be so elusive when we have been told by our spiritual leadership that Christ took care of everything? That Christ came to destroy the works of darkness so we could have life abundantly? That Christ defeated the devil once and for all? That the battle was over? If this is truly so, why has it seemed to so many that His incredible sacrifice and the shedding of His precious blood seemed to save us from our own sins just to bring us into a dark and fearsome battle with satanic forces bent on destroying us?

Consider the following verses carefully. Colossians 2:9-15 (AMP), *"For in Him* (Christ) *the whole fullness of Diety (the Godhead) continues to dwell in bodily form—giving complete expression of the divine nature. And you are in Him, made full and have come to fullness of life—in Christ you too are filled with the Godhead: Father, Son and Holy Spirit, and reach full spiritual stature. And He is the Head of all rule and authority— of every angelic principality and power. . . . And you, who were dead in trespasses and in the uncircumcision of your flesh—your sensuality, your sinful carnal nature—God brought to life together with Christ, having (freely) forgiven us all our transgressions; having cancelled and blotted out and wiped away the handwriting of the note (or bond) with its legal decrees and demands, which was in force and stood against us—hostile to us. This (note with its regulations, decrees and demands) He set aside and cleared completely out of our way by nailing it to (His) cross. God disarmed the principalities and powers ranged against us and made a bold display and public example of them, in triumphing over them in Him and in it (the cross)."*

Even though He loves us very much, I'm sure God must sometimes listen to our prayers, our doubts, and our fears to say, *"My child, my child! What part of this don't you understand?"*

ALL of the fullness of the Godhead dwells in Christ
You and I are in Christ in ALL fullness of life
Christ has ALL rule and authority over ALL
angelic principalities and powers
God brought us ALL to life together with Christ
GOD forgave us ALL our transgressions
Cancelled out ALL decrees and demands against
us and hostile to us
God disarmed ALL principalities and powers
ranged against us
God made a public display and example of
ALL of them
Triumphing over ALL of them in Christ and
the Cross!

(What part of this don't you get?)

What do you have to "live up to" in order to actually assume this unbelievable position of being fully in Christ, who is fully in the Godhead, who has full rule and authority over your enemies, who has made it possible for God to fully forgive you for everything you have ever done wrong, while He has fully disarmed every ugly and nasty thing trying to set itself against you? Guess what? It is not what you have to "live up to" in order to get all that is promised here, it is what you "give up" to make room to receive what is promised.

You have to give up your pain, your past, your confusion, your doubt, your neediness, your guilt, your shame, your fears, along with your soul's belief that it alone must fix or bury whatever is seeming unfixable. I have found that nothing short of my praying the prayers of loosing to break the hold these emotions and wrong beliefs have in my soul has ever effectively cut them away from me. Oh, Lord, give me a renewed mind, a surrendered will, and healed emotions so that I can be all you have implanted in the Seed of promise within me.

Use The Truth To Get Free

We've all been taught from the pulpit, from television ministries, from books, and from home meetings that as a believer, if we faithfully pour the Word of God into ourselves, it will change our lives— seemingly all on its own. This is not always true. You must receive that Word, believe it is true, and come into right agreement with it to let it begin to change your life. Your born again spirit has no problem agreeing with the Word of God, probably loving to roll around in it like it was an oasis in the Sahara. However, until you have finally stripped your human soul of all its half-baked ideas about Jesus Christ and how you should relate to Him, it will be your unsurrendered soul that will accept bits and pieces of the Word and reject the parts it sees as threatening to its status quo.

The Word of God, no matter how faithfully you read it, can mean little to your defensive, self-protected, self-barricaded, self-fortressed soul! And if your unsurrendered soul continues to upstage your spirit for control of your life, it will keep your mind from being renewed by the beautiful Word. An unrenewed mind cannot come into perfect agreement with God's premises and promises. His promises are that He will work all things together for good if you love Him and are called according to His purposes. He's already positioned everything according to His will in heaven for you, a positioning that guarantees all will work out right.

God has already set His will for everything, everyone, every time, every place, in heaven. When you pray and bind yourself and others involved in a certain circumstance to God's will, God's will can be manifested on earth in the situation. Your right prayers become the instrument of the manifestation of His will. The reason things sometimes don't work out for us when we have prayed is almost always because we do not trust that He will always do what is right and best (i.e. what we think is best).

We are told in both the Old Testament and the New Testament to magnify the Lord. We truly do have a reflex reaction to problems that causes us to turn our magnifying glasses on the circumstances and magnify them. We need to make sure what our built-in magnifying glass is magnifying Him. If we focus on praying to tell Him what He should do, the negative circumstances keep whining and growling around around in our lives. Been there, done that, bought the t-shirt and gave it away before I got back home. We don't have to go there anymore!

5

It's Not About You Anymore

Let's Get the Fruit Out

The world does not understand the things of the Spirit of God, but it does understand the fruit of the Spirit translated through a surrendered soul radiating love, kindness, peace, and joy. These spiritual attributes are expressed to others by your words and actions. Do you realize that every moment you are in the presence of others, you are either moving them towards or away from wanting what you have? In Galatians 5:22-23 (NKJ), we read: "The fruit of the Spirit is love, joy, peace, longsuffering, kindness, goodness, faithfulness, gentleness, self-control. Against such there is no law." So, just how fruity are you, little one?

The fruit of the Spirit are sweet products of Christ's goodness within His Seed of life in a Christian. Let's briefly look at each one.

Love Fruit

The Apostle Paul gives a wonderful list of the specifications of the spiritual fruit of love in 1 Corinthians 13:4-7, *"Love is patient, love is kind, and is not jealous; love does not brag and is not arrogant, does not act unbecomingly; it does not seek its own, is not provoked, does not take into account a wrong suffered, does not rejoice in unrighteousness, but rejoices with the truth; bears all things, believes all things, hopes all things, endures all things"* (NAS). If these attributes are not flowing through your actions towards others, then you have some clogs in your soul. You have been learning what to do about that.

Rethink the above verse the next time you say, "Oh, yes, I love him/her. I just find them very difficult to be around, so I stay away from them." Have you been unceasingly patient and kind towards them, having no unbecoming attitudes or thoughts? Are you seeking their best, refusing to be provoked by any of their actions? Are you believing and hoping for their best? Are you enduring everything they might say or do to you? True love does.

Joy Fruit

Do others always remark that you are so full of joy? Jesus spoke to His followers, recorded in John 15:10-11, *"If ye keep my commandments, ye shall abide in my love; even as I have kept my Father's commandments, and abide in his love. These things have I spoken unto you, that my joy might remain in you, and that your joy might be full"* (KJV). John said (3 John 1:4), *"I have no greater joy than to hear that my children walk in truth"* (KJV). If you research the word joy in the New Testament, you will find that the epistle writers often refer to their joy as coming from seeing success, growth, and joy in others. Are you spreading joy to others?

Peace Fruit

What does the Word say about this sometimes elusive fruit of the Spirit called peace? Psalms 119:165, *"Great peace have they which love thy law: and nothing shall offend them"* (KJV). Isaiah 26:3, *"Thou wilt keep him in perfect peace, whose mind is stayed on thee: because he trusteth in thee"* (KJV). Jesus said (John 14:27), *"Peace I leave with you, my peace I give unto you: not as the world giveth, give I unto you. Let not your heart be troubled, neither let it be afraid"* (KJV). James 3:17-18, *"The wisdom that is from above is first pure, then peaceable, gentle, and easy to be entreated, full of mercy and good fruits, without partiality, and without hypocrisy. And the fruit of righteousness is sown in peace of them that make peace"* (KJV).

These verses speak of the truth of peace from above. Do you bring peace into other peoples' troubled souls?

Longsuffering Fruit

Longsuffering means great and enduring patience, patience that goes on and on. To be humanly patient is one thing, but to be patient with great endurance is a truly divine fruit. Had God not been longsuffering towards me, I can only wonder where I would be now. Thank you, Lord (pass it on, reader!). In Ephesians 4:1-3, Paul beseeched the Ephesian church to *"walk worthy of the vocation wherewith ye are called, with all lowliness and meekness, with <u>longsuffering</u>, forbearing one another in love; endeavouring to keep the unity of the Spirit in the bond of peace"* (KJV). First Timothy 1:16 tells us Paul said, *"I was shown mercy so that in me, the worst of sinners, Christ Jesus might display his <u>unlimited patience</u>* (longsuffering KJV) *as an example for those who would believe on him and receive eternal life"* (NIV).

The Greek word for longsuffering is *makrothumia* (Strong's/Thayers #3115) meaning patience, endurance, constancy, steadfastness, perseverance, forbearance, longsuffering, slowness in avenging wrongs. Slow down, friend, and let the fruit of patience blossom in your life.

Kindness Fruit

We are told to be kind to both those in the world and those who are our spiritual brethren. In the Greek, the word kind/kindness is *chrestotes* (Strong's/Thayers #5544), meaning moral goodness, integrity, and kindness. The spiritual fruit of kindness never has an ulterior motive or a hidden agenda and always benefits others. Luke 6:35 says to even *"love your enemies, and <u>do good, and lend, expecting nothing in return; and your reward will be great</u>, and you will be sons of the Most High; for He Himself is <u>kind</u> to ungrateful and evil (men)"* (NAS). Ephesians 4:32, *"And be ye <u>kind</u> one to another, tenderhearted, forgiving one* *another, even as God for Christ's sake hath forgiven you"* (KJV). Be kind to someone today, someone who needs to see how kindness works.

Goodness Fruit

Most references in the Bible regarding goodness speak of the goodness (kindness, gentleness, patience) of God towards us. We should always treat others with goodness borne straight from the Seed of His Son's goodness rooted down in us. Psalm 31:19 praises God, *"Oh how great is thy goodness, which thou hast laid up for them that fear thee; which thou hast wrought for them that trust in thee before the sons of men!"* (KJV).

Share the goodness of God with others that they might know He is for them, and not against them.

Faithfulness Fruit

Faithfulness is the attribute of one in whom faith can be placed. The Greek word for faith in the verses speaking of faithfulness is *pistos* (Strong's/Thayers #4103) meaning trustworthy, faithful, one who can be relied on. In Daniel 6:4 (NAS), we read, *"The commissioners and satraps began trying to find a ground of accusation against Daniel in regard to government affairs; but they could find no ground of accusation or (evidence of) corruption, inasmuch as he was faithful, and no negligence or corruption was (to be) found in him."* The one who is faithful is a good witness for his Lord, for his character is solid and able to be relied upon.

Gentle Fruit

The original Greek *epieikeia* describes the gentleness of Christ as a suitable, fair attitude of clemency. Christ's gentleness was not necessarily a quiet, shy reaching out to touch lives. It was a strong loving attitude of *clemency*—compassion, forgiveness, forbearance, lenience, and mercy. Second Timothy 2:24-26 records Paul saying, *"The Lord's bond-servant must not be quarrelsome, but be kind to all, able to teach, patient when wronged, with gentleness correcting those who are in opposition, if perhaps God may grant them repentance leading to the knowledge of the truth, and they may come to their senses (and escape) from the snare of the devil, having been held captive by him to do his will"* (NAS).

Self-Control/Temperance Fruit

Second Peter 1:5-8 tells us: *"Giving all diligence, add to your faith virtue; and to virtue knowledge; and to knowledge temperance; and to temperance patience; and to patience godliness; and to godliness brotherly kindness; and to brotherly kindness charity. For if these things be in you, and abound, they make you that ye shall neither be barren nor unfruitful in the knowledge of our Lord Jesus Christ"* (KJV). Temperance is translated here from the Greek word *egkrateia*. It is the virtue of one who masters his soulish desires and passions and his sensual appetites.

Are You Still Reading?

Every one of these spiritual fruit exists within that Seed of life planted within you at the point of your new

110

birth. You don't have to find them, research them, learn them, or even grow them yourself. But you do need to unclog the riverbed of your soul to let them flow purely out of you to a world that desperately needs to see them manifested in the life of a child of God. The fruit of the Spirit are not spirits, i.e. spirit of joy, spirit of self-control, etc. They are special spiritual endowments deposited into the renewed spirit of the Christian. Your spirit's reservoir is chock full, literally bobbing with gorgeous, luscious fruit <u>right now</u>! If this fruit is not manifesting itself in the natural realm of your relationships with others, your soul has choked off its outward flow.

What to do? Loose, strip, smash, crush, and shatter all wrong beliefs, wrong attitudes, and wrong stronghold thinking patterns that have created the clog. In logging days of yore, the floating of harvested logs down rivers could create a log jam that clogged the river's flow. The old-time loggers often dynamited these log jams. Use your key of loosing and blast open your soul's attitude/belief jam—turn it into a flow of luscious fruit to bless the world. Stunted, tiny fruit in a Christian's life means largeness in the soul. God wants maxi-Christians with fully surrendered souls popping out fat fruit!

Reactions Tell the Real Truth

Have you ever walked out of a church service and been blindsided by someone who hates you? This person spewed venom and anger in your face, and all of your self-perceived spiritual fruit got blown away. Were you really filled with fruit of the Spirit? Or had your soul been self-enforcing appropriate behaviors to convince

111

you that you were doing just fine in your spiritual growth? Your emotions will masquerade, your mind will trick you, your self-will will behave, and the enemy will gleefully capitalize on their games.

When you are overflowing with the fruit of the Spirit, you can walk out of church, be blindsided by someone who hates you, and respond with a full course of the fruit of the Spirit instead of reactions from your unsurrendered soul. You will be able to sincerely smile, offer a hug, give your coat, buy them lunch, and rent a taxi to take them home! The fruit of the Spirit are given to believers to serve other with Christ-like attitudes flowing from their surrendered souls. The fruit of the Spirit makes sweet servings.

The Third Challenge of the Unsurrendered Soul

In an earlier chapter, I mentioned two challenges that come from unsurrendered souls with regard to Christians' self-will/free will. Actually there are three. Every nine months or so, I receive a rash of stronghold reactions to page 117 of *Shattering Your Strongholds* with regard to my statements on unforgiveness. Strongholds in our unsurrendered souls are far more powerful in controlling our thoughts, feelings, and actions than most Christians have any idea of or are willing to consider.

Hard truth goes "down" better when it is mixed with grace, but even with all of the grace in the universe, believers who cling to their unforgiveness will not be allowed to work out this sin in heaven. Sin is never neutralized by grace. The deserved consequences of ongoing sin may be held in abeyance by grace while the Christian is working out his or her own carnal mindsets, but sin must be repented of, given up, turned away from, and forgiven by the blood of Christ here on earth. Someone once said to me, "What if Jesus Christ was coming back in five minutes and I had unforgiveness in my soul. Are you saying I wouldn't get to go with Him?" I replied that those would probably become the most INTENSE FIVE MINUTES this person would ever experience in his entire life, just because God did want him to go with Him!

Christ died a brutal physical death in the form of the Son of Man to see that we could be forgiven for all we had previously done to reject the Father's love. We are only asked to die to our souls' desire to withhold forgiveness from others who have hurt us. Why is this so hard? I believe the reason is a hidden agenda of hoping to somehow avenge unresolved issues still burning hot within the soul.

I think God will push unforgiving Christians into very intense situations (if necessary) to get them to release grudges, offenses, and unforgiveness. The Holy Spirit will work and work with believers to get them to forgive, dispensing great spiritual and emotional pressure upon the soul of one who resists. Anyone who can hold out against this pressure year after year runs the risk of ending up with unforgiveness hardwired into their souls, a state dangerously close to having a seared conscience.

How can we refuse to forgive another person if we have asked for and received the forgiveness Christ purchased for us on the Cross? Can Christ's sacrifice ever be seen as too small to enable us to forgive what has been done to us? Salvation of our spirits is definitely not by works, of the law, or otherwise. But the salvation of our souls requires a release of every wrong pattern of thinking and all unforgiveness, or we find ourselves expecting God to negate one of the requests in the The Lord's Prayer, *"Forgive us as we forgive others."* Our request would have to be, "Forgive us in spite of our not forgiving others." There are consequences to disobeying any command Christ gave to us. Some are temporal, some are eternal.

Three-Question Quiz

There are three questions I ask people who say they have forgiven others who have negatively impacted their lives. Keep these points in your mind: unforgiveness is not an unhealed hurt needing healing, an unmet need that needs to be met, or an unresolved issue needing resolution. Unforgiveness is a rebellious, disobedient attitude of an unsurrendered soul that needs to be loosed along with the wrong beliefs and patterns of thinking that try to justify its existence.

The first thing I ask people is can they ask God to bless the ones they say they have forgiven. Most people think for a moment or two and reply, "Yes, I could do that."

Then I ask: Can they ask God to give the persons they say they have forgiven a double portion of the blessings they have asked to receive for themselves? This usually requires a few moments more of thinking than the first question. Most end up replying, "Yes, I think I could do that."

Then I ask the third question: Can they ask God to use them in any way He desires to see that the double portion blessing is given to those they say they have forgiven? Many times there is somewhat of a sheepish reaction at this point, "I'm not sure I can pray that." Often truth emerges from denial according to how you ask the questions. A Christian who has truly forgiven would have no problem in being used to double bless someone they had released from all accountability for past offenses. Isn't that why we are so blessed by what Christ has done for us? We've been released from all accountability for our past offenses against God!

To reach this final freedom requires us to give up all rights to withhold any form of grace and mercy and forgiveness from anyone. Once we have determined that this is what we are going to do no matter how much it might hurt, the empowerment comes down from heaven to help us do it. The resulting freedom is unbelievable, and you may find that many unanswered prayers are suddenly answered, too. Mark 11:25-26 records Jesus as saying, *"When ye stand praying, forgive, if ye have ought against any: that your Father also which is in heaven may forgive you your trespasses. But if ye do not forgive, neither will your Father which is in heaven forgive your trespasses"* (KJV). Forgiveness is truly a breakthrough principle for peace, productive prayer, and promises produced!

One final paragraph on this from Matthew Henry's Commentary and one from Adam Clarke's Commentary with regard to the passage of the Lord's Prayer as written in Matthew 6:12:

"As we forgive our debtors is not a plea of merit, but a plea of grace. Those that come to God for the forgiveness of their sins against him, must make conscience of forgiving those who have offended them, else they curse themselves when they say the Lord's prayer. . . . we must forbear, and forgive, and forget the affronts put upon us, and the wrongs done us. This is a

moral qualification for pardon and peace; it encourages (us) to hope that God will forgive us . . . an evidence to us that he has forgiven us (is His) having wrought in us the condition of forgiveness" (from Matthew Henry's Commentary).

"As we forgive our debtors was a maxim among the ancient Jews, that no man should lie down in his bed without forgiving those who had offended him. That man condemns himself to suffer eternal punishment, who makes use of this prayer with revenge and hatred in his heart. He who will not attend to a condition so advantageous to himself (remitting a hundred pence to his debtor, that his own creditor may remit him 10,000 talents) is a madman, who, to oblige his neighbour to suffer an hour, is himself determined to suffer everlastingly! This condition of forgiving our neighbour, though it cannot possibly merit anything, yet it is that condition without which God will pardon no man" (from Adam Clarke Commentary).

Joseph Knew

Joseph (one of Rachel's two sons by Jacob) was not liked by his other brothers. His father clearly preferred him, making a splendid coat of many colors for him to wear. At a fairly young age, Joseph received a prophetic dream from the Lord, and then told his family that the dream showed them bowing down to him. This greatly angered his brothers, who had no intentions of ever bowing down to their younger brother.

In Genesis 37:20, the brothers tending the sheep in the fields saw Joseph approaching them and began to plot as to how they could murder him. In verse 26, Judah talked his brothers into selling Joseph to a caravan of Ishmaelite merchants headed for Egypt instead of killing him. The brothers agreed that if Joseph became a slave in Egypt, he would never get anyone to bow down to him. In verse 31, the brothers told their father that Joseph had been killed by a wild animal and then gave him Joseph's coat which had been dipped into the blood of a goat. Jacob was inconsolable in his grief over the loss of his beloved Joseph.

The Ishmaelite merchants sold Joseph to Potiphar, one of Pharoah's officials in Egypt. Potiphar noted that the Lord made everything Joseph did to prosper (Genesis 39:3), so he made Joseph overseer of his house. One day Potiphar's wife propositioned Joseph, asking him to have sex with her. He refused, but she persisted. When the men of the house were in the fields, she grabbed Joseph's garment as he ran from her. She called the men, telling them Joseph had tried to rape her. Potiphar became enraged and threw Joseph into the king's prison.

God's divine methods often seem to contradict a tidy path towards His end purposes, yet His ways always accomplish exactly what He wants. One day the palace's chief butler and chief baker made Pharoah angry and he threw them into his prison. Joseph interpreted their dreams for them, which came to pass. When they were released he asked that they remember him, as he was in prison unjustly. Then Joseph's dream interpretations came to pass in full—the baker was hanged, but the butler was restored to service with the king. However, the butler forgot him, and Joseph languished in the prison for two years.

Pharoah had a dream which deeply troubled him, but none of his magicians could interpret it. The chief butler told Pharoah how Joseph had interpreted his dream, as well as the baker's. Joseph was brought before the Pharoah and interpreted his dream as meaning that seven years of plenty were coming and should be stored up, because seven years of famine would follow. The Pharoah was so impressed with Joseph's understanding, he made Joseph head over all of the plans for storing up against the famine.

When the famine came, Joseph's brothers came to Egypt to buy corn to feed their families. Knowing what this unknown powerful man could do to them, Joseph's unsuspecting brothers bowed down to him in fear. Joseph told his brothers to come close to him and he said, *"I am Joseph your brother, whom you sold into Egypt; but now do not be distressed and disheartened, or vexed and angry with yourselves because you sold me here, for God sent me ahead of you to preserve life . . . God sent me before you to preserve you . . . So now it was not you who sent me here, but God"* (Genesis 45:4, 7, 8, AMP). Even when falsely accused of rape and left in prison, Joseph managed to stay in step with God's plans and purposes for him. Joseph may have struggled with his soul during those years in prison, but there was no oversight on God's part. God did not say, "Now where did I put that fellow? I know it was somewhere in Egypt, but I just can't think where." No, God was accomplishing something in Joseph, and the others as well, during those seemingly unproductive years.

We do not know what God is doing most of the time, we must just realize that He is always doing something to benefit everyone. We must learn to align our will with His, regardless of how futile circumstances around us seem. Over and over, God's people have blown opportunities for God to place them in positions of great influence with people in high places. Who would believe that God would allow one of His children to be sold into slavery, falsely accused of rape, imprisoned for years, all to create a position of influence with a world leader for the preserving of the lives of God's own people? He's God and we must learn to let Him color outside the lines of our understanding so He can position us however He wants, wherever He wants.

How easy it would have been for Joseph to want to destroy his brothers who had tried to destroy him. How easy it would have been for Joseph to say, "You're bowing down to me now, aren't you? I told you so, but you wouldn't listen. Well, you can just go back to Canaan and starve!" Joseph never wavered from God's will, regardless of whether he thought God had wavered or not. Again, God's divine methods may seem to contradict a tidy path towards His end purposes, yet His ways are always working even as though from a distance to accomplish exactly what He wants.

What Could Your Earthly Destiny Be?

The Message gives us a wonderful expanded understanding of the fruit of the Spirit in our lives (Galatians 5:22-26). *"What happens when we live God's way? He brings gifts into our lives, much the same way that fruit appears in an orchard—things like affection for others, exuberance about life, serenity. We develop a willingness to stick with things, a sense of compassion in the heart, and a conviction that a basic holiness permeates things and people. We find ourselves involved in loyal commitments, not needing to force our way in life, able to marshal and direct our energies wisely. Legalism is helpless in bringing this*

119

about; it only gets in the way. Among those who belong to Christ, everything connected with getting our own way and mindlessly responding to what everyone else calls necessities is killed off for good—crucified. Since this is the kind of life we have chosen, the life of the Spirit, <u>let us make sure that we do not just hold it as an idea in our heads or a sentiment in our hearts, but work out its implications in every detail of our lives</u>. This means we will not compare ourselves with each other as if one of us were better and another worse. We have far more interesting things to do with our lives."

Yes, we do! Like walking, stomping, marching, and dancing forth on our destiny paths. We have a destiny promise within us that is going to burst forth even if it has to break the vessel it is planted in. God's plans are so much higher than our finite and often petty little plans. His plans for us must burst apart our boundaries, our preconceived ideas, our comfort zones, or we will be miserable. Totally miserable, just like an elephant with a breech birth blockage of overdue quadruplets! Ooooooouch! (I know elephants don't have quadruplets, but I'm trying to convey the concept of serious consequences here.)

God has "arranged" His will in heaven to be manifested according to right prayers from earth. Jesus said we are to pray that the Father's will would be done on earth as it is in heaven (The Lord's Prayer, Matthew 6:10). This is not a calling forth, rather this is a right agreement alignment with His will to see His purposes transferred from the supernatural realm of heaven into the natural realm here on earth. God has always known what He intended to happen in our lives and in the lives of others that He expects us to pray right prayers for. We come into alignment with this through the dismantling of our unsurrendered souls' agendas by binding and loosing prayers. Or, we can cross our legs and try not to birth those elephant quadruplets as God breaks up the breech defense our souls are trying to keep in place.

Family Dynamics

I come from a family where everybody is a chief—no Indians, just chiefs. We experience some very dynamic family dynamics—dynamics being *continuous interacting forces within a group*. That's us, all right—heavy on the forces and heavy on the continuous. Most family dynamics begin over an upset of the balance of power among hurting souls. Then a second dynamic to change the focus enters and you find yourself embroiled in emotional discussions about things that have nothing to do with where it all started. Once a family is rolling this rapidly, everyone seems to get drawn in and it's downhill from there. God has been teaching me about making a paradigm shift in my thinking when viewing such negative situations. I believe that many times people want a way out of a negative situation, but do not know how to withdraw without losing face or being embarrassed.

Christians can become that doorway if they are willing to. It is only hard to do this when you have unhealed hurts and unmet needs that cause you to fear losing face or being embarrassed yourself. When you have bound your will to the will of God and loosed all hindrances within your soul blocking your own healing, you move closer to becoming that doorway. Not a door mat, but a doorway. However, if a doormat is what Jesus needs you to be for a hurting family member, the fruit of love will immediately try to flow out of your spirit to obey His request. If it can't get out, it is because of the hardness of your own heart. Our difficult relationships are usually difficult because of <u>our feelings</u> towards the other person.

Some Christians tell me that they love their families, they just don't like them. What a deception. First Corinthians 13 was not put into the Bible because it makes a really neat wall plaque to hang in your bathroom. **First Corinthians 13 is the pattern of love**. Only by binding my will to God's will and my mind to the mind of Christ, by loosing my soul's finite interpretation of circumstances and issues, can I ever really see what is going on in dynamics with difficult people. Then I can become a door for them to exit the dynamic. This prayer will help it begin to happen:

Family Dynamics

Lord, thank you that you have adopted us and made us a part of the biggest and best family ever—the family of God! Let every one of us never forget that huge blessing and benefit. Let me never lose sight of the power of such a great gift because of the painful dynamics of my own human family. As we now move into the end times, many of our families are more confused and fragmented than ever. A perfect case scenario would be that each of us experienced all the nurturing, love, acceptance, mercy, and provision that we needed. The perfect case scenario would would be that we were never abused, neglected, betrayed, abandoned, rejected, ridiculed, wrongly accused, or misunderstood. Many of us never even got close to such perfect case scenarios, Lord, and we have been told we just need to "deal with it" and get on with our lives. Many have felt that such perfection could never be ours.

Dear Father God, you can redeem us with the blood of your precious Son from every terrible thing ever done to us, said about us, taken from us, or commited by us. I bind every wounded heart in every hurting family to the truth that you want to and will freely give all the nurturing, love, acceptance, mercy, and provision they can receive. You will never abuse, neglect, betray, abandon, or reject any one. You will never ridicule, belittle, wrongly accuse, or misunderstand any broken heart. The only thing preventing that from being our heritage right now is the unwillingness of our unsurrendered souls to trust and surrender our pain to you.

Lord, let my see the ones who have hurt me as having been hurt by others who were hurt by others. Let me understand that imperfect people create imperfect people. Let me be the one who stops the cycle in my family. I bind myself to your will, God. I bind my mind to the mind of Christ. I bind myself to the truth that you can restore and make all things new if I will let you. I loose from myself all old patterns of thinking, wrong attitudes, the effects and influences of wrong agreements, and the power of the hard, cruel words that have been spoken to me. I loose these things from every member of my family.

*Lord, help me to understand that **I don't "have to go there" anymore** when old family dynamics begin to play out. I can be the one who uses the keys of the Kingdom to open up all of heaven's grace and mercy and blessing for my family. I can be their doorway out. And I will! Amen.*

Surface Judgments

I heard a minister tell of riding the subway when a father got on with three very wild and unruly children. The children were screaming and running, stepping on peoples' feet, as well as other irritating things. As the minister looked around the subway car, he realized that someone needed to do something before one of the less spiritual riders grabbed one of the kids. He slid over to the man who was staring blankly at his hands, oblivious to his children, and said firmly, "Sir, I think you should discipline your children. They are upsetting everyone on the car."

The man looked up with red eyes and wiped his face. Focusing on his children, he said, "I'm sorry. I will. I guess they are reacting the only way they know how. They just watched their mother die back there in the hospital."

The minister suddenly looked at the children and their father from a whole new perspective. Now he felt a deep compassion for them, where before he had been irritated at the father's lack of concern. We must learn how to see beyond the surface appearances of peoples' lives before we come to conclusions about them. Only then can we embrace God's divine understanding of any human situation. We need to make up our minds that regardless of what wrong doorway another insensitive or angry soul challenges us to step through, no matter how familiar those doorways might look—we can always say, "Nope, I don't think so. I'm not going there."

Blessed at the Bowery Mission in Manhattan

In October of 1997, Evelyn and I traveled through ten states in six-and-a-half weeks. I may be height enhanced, but I'm definitely geographically impaired. I plotted out a crazy trip across the United States from California to Idaho to Pennsylvania to Illinois to Connecticut to New Jersey to New York to Kentucky to Texas to Florida and then back to California. By the time we arrived in New Jersey (our fifth stop) to meet and stay with my publisher and his wife, Guy and Kitty Morrell of Bridge-Logos Publishers, we were already burning out. We walked into the publishing house around 4:30 p.m. to be confronted by four men we had never met. These men said, "You have to hurry and change your clothes right now. We have you booked into the Bowery Mission in Manhattan at 7:00 o'clock. Hurry, hurry."

My tired body and groggy soul began to rebel. I heard all kinds of thoughts rumbling up from Soul Central and they sounded like this, "Excuse me? I don't think so. No one asked me if I wanted to preach at the Bowery Mission. I've been all over the United States and I'm tired and I don't want to preach tonight."

Before I could actually verbalize these thoughts, I heard a small voice in my head say, *"Did you get up this morning and bind your will to my will?"*

"Yes," I muttered back unhappily, thinking to myself that I hadn't dreamed it would mean this was in the offing when I did it. Surely God didn't expect me to do this, did He? He did. The four men were fairly jumping up and down now, trying to get me to get back in the car and go to the Morrell's nearby house and change clothes.

I hard the little voice again, *"Did you get up this morning and bind your will to my will?"* I groaned and turned to Evelyn and told her we had to go change

125

clothes. So off we rushed, changed our clothes, and I stopped to make a quick phone call. I had heard of the streets of Manhattan down in the Bowery. I frankly was a little unsure of what to expect. So, I called California to get some prayer support. Due to the time difference of three hours, everyone I knew was at work. I called my Aunt Mildred, but she was out. So I called my mother, although I knew she would worry about me going into New York. Actually my mother worries about me all the time, but she will pray when I remind her that it is more productive. My mother was out, but my father answered the phone.

My father has always been my difficult person in the family. We have had some serious relationship dynamics to overcome, but as we both grew older and mellowed, it became a little easier to interact. He had never told me I was special or that he loved me, unless he grunted back, "Me, too," if I told him I loved him. But I was desperate for a prayer partner, and while my father did pray to God from time to time, he was adamant that he didn't believe in this Jesus fellow. Still, a prayer is a prayer if you're desperate enough, right? So I asked him if he would pray. Surprisingly enough, he said yes. So I asked him to pray right now. He said okay. So I asked him to pray out loud. He said okay and began to pray.

"God, take care of my daughter. She's special and I love her. Amen."

I was completely shocked, and I burst into tears. Here I was, 56 years old, and my father had just told God I was special and said that he loved me for the first time. I wailed, "You made me cry!"

My father said, "Yeah, I did. Bye!" and quickly hung up.

Then it was time to rush back to the publishing house. The next thing I knew, we were careening through the Holland Tunnel, Evelyn and I and four men we had never met before. I looked at her and said, "If we're not on an adventure with God here, we're in big trouble." I decided I had better jot down a few notes for my sermon, a few ideas on how to teach the street people of Manhattan about binding and loosing. Lord, have mercy on me, was all I could think.

When we pulled up to the Bowery Mission, I was aware of the darkness around us as I got out of the car. We walked inside and met briefly with the staff of the Mission. I asked the director how long I had to preach and he said, "Twenty minutes."

I immediately protested that this was impossible. There was no way I could teach them anything meaningful in twenty minutes. I'll preach two to three hours if someone will listen. All of my protests were to no avail, I had twenty minutes, period. I was informed that these people had come in off the cold streets to eat, and they couldn't go into the dining room until I was through—I would be lucky to hold their attention twenty minutes. My soul began to snarl, "I didn't ask for this gig, I didn't plan on it, I can't do it, I don't want to." I briefly thought again about rebelling and once more the little voice in my head said, *"Did you get up this morning and bind your will to my will?"* It was clear I wasn't going to get any sympathy from God!

The next thing I knew we were in the chapel and I was sitting on the platform behind a beautiful, hand-carved pulpit that I later learned Abraham Lincoln had preached from. The chapel itself was long and narrow with high gothic style ceilings. Perhaps 100 or more people were sitting in the pews. I was clutching my little cheat sheet of notes and wondering how far I would get with them when I heard, "Let's welcome Rev. Liberty Savard." I walked to the pulpit and God said, *"Throw away those notes. I want you to teach about Rahab the harlot."*

"Rahab? Lord!" I urgently murmured, "I can't preach about a prostitute in here. Probably half of them are prostitutes." There was no answer, and I knew better than to try to rebel again. So I threw my pathetic little notes down and began to preach about Rahab the harlot. I told how God saw the intent of her heart and her desire to meet the God who had been killing kings and parting seas and delivering His people out of Egypt. He marked her as His and began to use her right in the middle of her wrong environment to change the destiny of history. I got so into the story, I forgot to look at my watch. I was only looking at their faces and the attitudes of their bodies as they leaned forward on the pews ahead of them, listening carefully to every word I was saying.

Suddenly I looked at my watch and I had been preaching 45 minutes. I wrapped everything up quickly and gave an altar call. About a third of the people came forward and we went down among them and prayed and cried with them. Then I walked down the aisle of the chapel and shook hands with the people who were smiling and thanking me for the message. About half way down the aisle, a troubled man called out a rather threatening question. A big black brother turned around and grabbed him by his lapels, appearing to lift him right off the floor as he growled, "Don't talk to the preacher woman like that, you hear!" I felt completely safe.

No one seemed to want to leave, and the kitchen staff were peeking into the chapel to see what was keeping the people, for it was obvious the meeting was over. Finally the people began to drift in to their dinner. The staff of the Mission and the four men I had gone there with all came and said that they had never heard a message like that preached there. One of the staff said, "I've worked here sixteen years, and I've never seen them so attentive. Most preachers come in here and recycle their Sunday sermons, but you preached right into the needs of their hearts."

Why was I so anointed that night? Because for the first time in my life, I had preached under the double blessing of my natural father and my heavenly Father.

If I had rebelled against the promise I had made God that morning when I bound my will to His will in prayer, I would have never made that phone call to California. I would have never heard my earthly father tell God that I was special and he loved me. Many of the things that we most desperately want to hear, or questions we want to have answered, are hidden in the darkness of the unknown. We will never find them on our own, but obedience to the will of God often places us in immediate proximity to them. I'm finding many of these hidden treasures in most unusual ways, and I am very aware that to rebel against anything God has especially set up for me might mean a treasure lost.

Some have come to me after this story and said, "That's fine for you. Your father was alive to say that. I never heard my father say it and he's dead now. So, where does that leave me?"

I softly answer, "That is finite thinking, human thinking without any divine influence. God knows what you need to know and He can get that information to you whether your father is dead or not. Let me tell you about my friend and his dead father."

My friend Roland lives in Texas and is a missionary to Mexico. All of Roland's efforts to tell his lawyer father about Christ were rebuffed for years. This important lawyer didn't have time for such stuff, and then one day he had a massive heart attack and died. Roland was devastated that he had never been able to share his faith with his father to the degree that he wanted to meet Jesus Christ. But Roland went on with his missionary work for God, still filled with faith in the goodness of God, although part of his heart was broken.

Later, Roland's wife was going through some boxes in the attic and a little booklet fell out of the box and onto the floor. Picking it up, she realized it was a copy of The Four Spiritual Laws. She looked inside and then rushed downstairs to find Roland. Opening the front cover, Roland saw that the salvation prayer had been filled out, every point checked off, with his father's signature on the bottom line. It was dated a short while before he died of the heart attack. Roland knew that of all the people who understood the importance of affixing his signature to a document, it was his father the lawyer. Roland had never faltered from his designated assignments for God, and God brought Roland what he needed to know most: proof of his father's salvation. God had brought forth a treasure for Roland, a treasure that had beem hidden in the unknown.

You will never know what hidden treasures are waiting for you in the darkness of the unknown paths He will ask you to walk—until you surrender and obey.

I Must Change

My ministry to my family is not to change them, but to change myself. If family members are holding on to their hurts and their offenses, any attempt to change them will be seen as attempts to inflict further hurt and offense. But if family members cannot fail to see how much God has changed us, they become positioned to reap answers from right prayers we begin to pray for them. We must stop praying prayers that tell God what He should do in each of their lives. We need to focus our prayers on loosing the effects and influences of wrong agreements off of them (spoken by others about them, spoken by others to them, spoken by us, spoken by themselves). Then we need to pray prayers of right agreement for them. The best one of all is that we bind them to the will of God and ask for His will to be done in their lives.

Every act, every word, every omission of our lives has great effect upon others around us. Ever since Adam and Eve blew it in the Garden of Eden, fathers and mothers have struggled with knowing how to raise their children the best way. In this past century, so many people have grown into adulthood and become parents themselves without ever having had good parenting skills modeled for them. Regardless of what romantic notions exist about being a parent, not every new father and mother knows how to be a good parent. We unfortunately learn so many wrong things, and even though we swear we will never treat our children like we were treated, we end up finding ourselves repeating the mistakes of our parents. We have had wrong seeds sown into our lives, and we in turn sow wrong seeds into the lives of our children. It is time for us to undo the wrong planting, to break and smash the effects of wrong agreements, and to bless our families. We have the keys to get it done.

6

Healing for Mankind

*"A calm and undisturbed mind and heart are the
life and health of the body, but envy, jealousy and wrath
are as rottenness of the bones"* (Proverbs 14:30, AMP).

Five Accidents?

In *Breaking the Power,* I tell the story of having
been in five rear-end automobile accidents in my life—
every one of them happening as I sat at the end of a line
of waiting traffic. I could not understand why this kept
happening to me until I finally identified being upset
with a different person around the time of two of the
accidents. Any time your body, soul, and spirit are out
of alignment with the will of God in any way, your body
and your soul are vulnerable to attack from natural
sources and supernatural sources. One fact I have seen
borne out in my life, although I don't have Scripture

for it, is that open doors of access in the soul give opportunity to the devil to set you up for accidents as well.

After the last accident, I found myself with an orthopedic specialist, a physical therapist, a chiropractor, and an ear, nose, and throat specialist because of vertigo. All four of the medical experts basically said the same thing, "You are going to be all right, but you have had so much repeated trauma to your upper body, you will never regain a full range of mobility. So, just accept it, adjust to it, and get on with your life the best you can." I was in a tremendous amount of pain when I was told this. When you are in a lot of pain, its very hard to want to resist accepting negative diagnoses from experts. You just want someone to fix the pain.

All four medical authorities said to me, "Go home and rest for two months. Cancel any traveling. It will be a long time before you feel like doing anything." So I went home, cancelled some out-of-state meetings, and crawled into my recliner. When I would get up out of the recliner, I would sort of shuffle slowly across the floor. Telephone ringing or fire alarm going off, it wouldn't have mattered. I was <u>moving slow</u>! Because I hurt. I really hurt. I don't like pain, I won't deny pain, I'll do anything to avoid pain So, my life went on hold for two months. Then one day, at the end of those two months, I slowly got up out of my recliner and raised my foot a little bit to take a tiny step. Suddenly I heard God say, ***"Get on with your life!"***

I snapped my drooping head up, straightened my back, froze in mid-air, and said, "<u>Yes, Sir</u>!" I had been hurt, I had been in pain, and I had needed to heal. But God obviously thought two months was long enough, and I realized I was at a crossroads. I could walk the road the doctors were telling me I had to walk, and I would have to walk out the natural results of that choice. But God seemed to be saying that I could choose to walk the other road, out of all of the preconceived ideas and conditioned responses I had learned in response to the pain of my accident and get on with my life.

So I took a small physical step and a giant paradigm shift of thinking step down the road of <u>His way</u>, and I've never looked back. I am not supposed to be able to move my head, neck, back, or shoulders with any kind of true freedom of mobility. But I now do just about anything I want to with no restriction of movement and only a rare twinge of discomfort from time to time.

I believe God said, *"Take that road called conventional wisdom, and you will walk out the natural results of your choice. Or take this road called divine wisdom, and I will heal you."* So, I walked out of the conventional path that four perfectly good doctors had carefully concluded to be my only choice. With all of the flying I do across the country, I do get stiff and go to a chiropractor every so often. I've had more than one say, "You really have an awful lot of scar tissue in your neck and back. It's amazing that you have such good mobility."

I just say, "Ain't God good!"

Moving On

A couple of years later, one night before I was to fly to Texas, I tangled with a drop-front dishwasher door and did a full back flip that would have made Mary Lou and Nadia proud! I remember briefly thinking while

135

upside down on my head in the corner of the kitchen, "God healed me after that last automobile accident, but this has probably undone everything!" When I focused on what was going on in my head, I caught myself and said, "No, it didn't. I will not agree with those negative thoughts, I am going to be fine." And I was, believe it or not.

I am really not a klutz, it has just been a strange few years for accidents. Earlier this year, I was in a motel bathroom in Ohio, showering in a very slippery tub before getting dressed to speak at a church service. Suddenly, without warning, I became like Bambi on ice—arms and legs flying everywhere. Once again, I landed upside down in a potential problem. I was delighted these words instantly flew out of my mouth: "Lord, I bind every single cell of my body to your will and purposes for my life. I bind every cell of my bones and muscles to your will." I repeated that prayer about five times, felt around for broken bones, disentangled myself, got onto my feet, and began to dress to go preach.

I had some discomfort in my right shoulder and arm after that, but it seemed to gradually be getting better. So, I did not let it affect what I needed to do. Then one day I stepped on a plastic bag and slid right into a door frame really hard. I hit right on that sore shoulder and arm. It hurt terribly! As I grabbed my shoulder and fell across my bed, I immediately said, "This is just God giving me a chiropractic adjustment to fix my shoulder. Thank you, God, thank you for doing this final adjustment on my shoulder." I don't care if I was actually right or not, but I am delighted to be viewing things from the perspective that God truly is in control of every single thing in my life. Even falling into a door frame.

I had stayed in agreement with the words that I prayed when I fell in the bathtub in Ohio, and I believed Christ had protected me and kept me whole. Evidently I just needed a chiropractic tweaking to set everything completely right! Who knew that door frame was so talented? Galatian 5:1 (KJV) tells us to hold to that which the Lord gives to us, *"Stand fast therefore in the liberty wherewith Christ hath made us free, and be not entangled again with the yoke of bondage."* To a child of God, an emergency should never be interpreted as impending disaster. It should simply signify a crossroads, another check point asking you: "Is your God able?" Yes, mine surely is.

Dis-Courage or En-Courage

Discourage and encourage are interesting words. When you dis-courage people, you take their courage away. When you en-courage people, you give them courage. Discouragement (symptom) comes when our expectations are confused, and we're not sure what the source of our problem is. The church world has become somewhat confused about the true sources of illness and physical infirmities of the human body.

Some time ago, a woman came into my office for counseling. She seemed rather uneasy, but finally she whispered, "I have a *thing* in my brain." I asked her to repeat what she had said. She whispered again, "The doctor says I have a *thing* in my brain." I asked her what kind of *thing.* She said, "You know, the t-word."

I said, "The t-word? Do you mean you have a tumor in your brain?" The poor woman flinched as if I had physically struck her. She nodded her head mutely. I said, "You have a tumor in your brain. Why can't you say that? If it is there, God knows it's there. Whispering won't change anything."

Now she was quite nervous, but she stammered out, "My pastor and our church prayer team said that I should not say the t-word because that gives glory to the devil. They said I should keep saying, 'Devil, you're a liar. Devil, you're a liar.' Please tell me, is that going to get me healed?"

"No," I replied, "I don't think that is going to get you healed. First of all, he knows he's a liar, so that is not exactly giving him unknown information. Secondly, if the doctors have actually found a tumor in your brain, that is a natural fact. Only God can effectively erase it with a supernatural act." Then I asked her if she believed God could heal. She did. So I asked her why He hadn't healed her.

She paused briefly and then replied, "Probably because I'm not a very worthy person." I told her that was a lie and we were going to loose it. I asked her again why God had not healed her. She replied, "Probably because I drink sometimes." I told her that drinking wasn't good for her, but was not why God hadn't healed her, and we were going to loose that wrong belief. I told her we were going to bind every cell of her body to the will and purposes of God, and we were going to loose the effects and influences of all wrong agreements off her as well as all diagnoses that did not line up with God's plans for her life and her destiny here on earth. We also loosed the reproductive ability of any alien, mutated cells in her body. Together we prayed the binding and loosing healing prayer.

She left my office looking like she had shed ten years of worry and fear. Within six months, I received an e-mail from her. She had just returned from seeing her doctor and he was amazed that a C.A.T. scan had just revealed the tumor had completely disappeared. Had that poor woman spend those six months walking around saying, "Devil, you're a liar," I believe there is a good chance she would have been dead before the six months were up. Why? Because she would have had to walk out the natural consequences of the natural fact of the tumor. Nothing she had been told to do had yet opened up and removed the negative wrong ideas and beliefs in her soul to make room to receive her supernatural healing.

Shortly thereafter, another woman came into my office for counseling. She told me that she had epilepsy. Then she said that following a service in her church, after all of the pastors and leaders had gone home, the deliverance "team" came up to her and told her that her epileptic seizures were demonic. Within minutes they had wrestled her to the floor, were pounding on her chest, and calling for demons to leave her body. She kept crying out to the people to leave her alone, attempting to break loose of them. Finally one of them said in disgust, "It is obvious you don't want to be delivered. You like having those demons in you." They let her up and walked away from her, leaving her devastated.

This woman asked me with all sincerity if I thought her epilepsy was demonic and if I thought she wanted demons inside of her. Did I believe she did not want to be healed? It is very hard to remain calm, non-judgmental, and non-critical at moments like that. Well meaning or not, these deliverance "specialists" had caused this woman a great deal of pain and grief. I assured her that I did not believe her epilepsy was demonic nor did she have demons inside of her. Together we prayed the binding and loosing prayers for her healing. The woman has since shown a remarkable physical improvement and had stopped taking the epilepsy medication.

Let's Get It Right

It is very difficult for finite thought processes (human sense and reasoning without any influence of the Holy Spirit) to understand why Christians can get devastating diseases and die. It is hard for believers to understand why Christians can exercise their faith with all their might, seemingly do all of the right things, yet divine healing does not come.

In God's Word, the Epistle of James asks (James 5:14, KJV), *"Is any sick among you? Let him call for the elders of the church; and let them pray over him, anointing him with oil in the name of the Lord. And the prayer of faith shall save the sick, and the Lord shall raise him up; and if he have committed sins, they shall be forgiven him. Confess your faults one to another, and pray one for another, that ye may be healed. The effectual fervent prayer of a righteous man availeth much."* This verse appears to be very straight forward with no mention of clauses or conditions here. So how can Christians be anointed with oil by the elders of the Church, confess their sins, be prayed over by mature intercessors, be quoting the Word on a daily basis, and still die?

How Much Faith Does a Dead Man Have?

I have heard ministers and evangelists say that

someone they prayed for was not healed because the afflicted one didn't have the faith to receive a healing. Lazarus was dead when he received his healing—how much faith can a dead person have? However, there is a small possibility that being dead meant he didn't have any doubt or disbelief, either. Poor Lazarus didn't have anything, he was dead.

What about the young man in Luke 7:12-15 whose body was being carried to his funeral on a bier. He had no faith—he was dead. There is no mention of his widowed mother (who was walking beside the bier) as having faith to believe for a miracle, either. We find no record of her asking Jesus to heal her only son, or of her expressing her faith in Him as the one who could heal. Yet her son, the dead man, was healed of the ultimate affliction—death.

How very, very hard it seems at times to understand what appears to be miracles for one who is prayed for and nothing for another who has been the recipient of countless peoples' intercession. What strange sort of unknown rules govern whether or not God will heal? This chapter is for those of you seeking healing for your own bodies, with a broader hope that you will also impart healing to others who are hurting and sick. Every one of you should be an instrument to impart God's grace, mercy, and healing power into the bodies of others! But you may need a paradigm shift in your thinking to become so.

Do you need to be in perfect health yourself to be used in prayer for healing of other afflicted bodies? No. That's a strange thing to finite thinking processes, but I have seen those who are crippled and bent impart healing to others' souls and bodies. You do need to have faith in God's promises to empower you to impart healing, coupled with knowledge and understanding about the power of the human soul—your soul and the souls of those who are sick. Faith alone does not always open the door to receiving God's answers. Understanding what might be blocking the receiving of a healing is very helpful.

Get On the Right Track

Many have taken strong-willed stands of faith on something they were convinced was surely the will of God. And they have stood and stood and stood—on the wrong spot. That is like taking your guaranteed ticket to ride the train and then waiting for it to show up beside the freeway ramp—lots of people going lots of places, but you're not. You're in the wrong spot. Faith alone can place great emphasis on something that may have absolutely nothing to do with God's plans for the present and the near future.

James 5:16 tells us that the effectual fervent prayer of a righteous man (or woman) avails much, accomplishes much, and is both powerful and effective. So, obviously it is a good thing if the one who is praying is righteous. The original Greek word *dikaios* (Strong's/ Thayers #1342, dik'-ah-yos) translated as "righteous" in James 5:16 means one whose way of thinking, feeling, and acting is wholly conformed to the will of God. What would keep you from thinking, feeling, and acting in a way that is wholly conformed to the will of God? Your own unrenewed mind, unhealed emotions, and unsurrendered will filled with the baggage and fears of a lifetime.

You are made up of body, soul, and spirit. The most ideal way to receive your healing is when all three parts of your makeup are in total agreement with God regarding His will for your life. Your unsurrendered soul:

- Creates conflict with your regenerated spirit's desire to believe and act upon everything God has promised to you in His Word,

- Creates open doors for the devil's attacks upon your body,

- Protects your wrong patterns of thinking, wrong beliefs, half-truths, and generational-bondage thinking about your physical health.

Wounded and Messy

When wounded, fearful, angry people with messy lives are coming into the Church today seeking answers to hard questions, spiritual leaders are struggling with issues not seemingly found in any tidy list of scriptural answers. It is becoming more and more of a dilemma of how to take wounded, traumatized, fearful people of today past their bondages of deep grief, fear, anger, and violation. God requires a voluntary submitting of all of the soul's defense systems before He will freely enter into the inner depths of each one of us. Unless this happens, permanent victory and healing will never be achieved. Temporary victories may take place, but the sources of the pain and fear and vulnerability to infirmity will still be in place.

Hallelujah, this is not a terminal state of being. I believe we could empty the mental hospitals, especially of everyone who has ever had any knowledge of the Lord Jesus Christ, with the keys of the Kingdom. The mind that is shut down is a mind no longer capable of dealing with what it perceives as the threat of harsh reality. This is a mind desperately in need of someone to step into the gap between it and its destiny of wholeness and restoration, by binding it to the mind of Christ—by binding it to the truth of God's Word which will bring it freedom—by binding it to the restoration of Christ's life in it, it's hope of glory—by loosing the effects and influences of word curses, wrong agreements, wrong covenants, and wrong vows from it—by loosing the hold of the wrong ideas, beliefs, attitudes, and patterns it has collected and accepted as its truth—and by loosing the strongholds protecting all of these bondages.

We have had testimonies come in from different parts of the world saying that the praying of binding and loosing prayers over people who had depression, fear, worry, schizophrenia, dementia, confusion, and other mental bondages, had produced great improvement and complete healing in some cases. These prayers have been prayed in agreement with others, individually, with the prayer team in our office, sometimes as a result of our office and our intercessors praying over written prayer requests we have received in the mail. We have received testimonies of whole families praying the binding and loosing prayers for loved ones in mental hospitals, loved ones whose minds had been pronounced as beyond cure. These same loved ones walked out of those hospitals whole and ready for life following the intense binding and loosing prayers that were prayed for them.

God has no investment in letting His people waste away in mental hospitals. He gets no glory from His people being trapped within the bondages of their own minds. But often these wounded minds are incapable of effecting their own breaking of the bondages. This is why we need each other. When a mind has shut down, we must see it as a wounded soldier fallen on a battlefield. Every one of us needs to be ready to put our own comfort, safety, and integrity on the line to get that soldier pulled into a safe foxhole while we call out for the greatest medic of all, Jesus Christ, to come and heal. We have learned, instead, to send a little money, say a little prayer, look the other way, and get on with our own lives that seem dangerously near overload. I once heard a pastor, whose church was in a rather rundown part of the city, say this: "If we don't watch out, the world is going to try to suck us dry with its needy and its poor and hungry. We have Christians bringing resources for the Kingdom in the front door, while the food lines and charity cases are draining everything we have right out the back door. We have to learn to be smarter and make sure we have all that we need to stay strong."

That almost sounds like it makes sense, doesn't it? But it is a terrible lie. That kind of thinking causes a church to turn in on itself, just like an ingrown toenail. Ingrown toenails are very painful, often becoming infected, and eventually causing the foot to be unable to walk. God's economic processes work best when no one tries to hoard His manna. God has told me that the ministry work and outreaches He tells me to enact will always have the resources necessary as long as I never try to hold onto any of the money He sends through my hands.

We have been so taught that we must be good stewards that we sometimes forget that a steward is generally a slave or an employee, following orders of a master or an employer. A good steward works for someone else, someone else who makes the final decisions. Our Master Employer is God himself. A pretty good representation of His orders seems to be found in Romans 15:1-2 (NIV), *"We who are strong ought to bear with the failings of the weak and not to please ourselves. Each of us should please his neighbor for his good, to build him up."*

Belief Must Act

Our oldest and deepest unmet needs, unhealed hurts, and unresolved issues are three areas of need, pain, and confusion—all sources of pain, fear, and vulnerability to natural diseases and spiritual attacks of the enemy. The most earnest intercessory prayer can be prayed in a "shotgun mode" when one is not praying specifically for God to get into the hidden areas of the soul's darkest hiding places.

To believe is more than just a mental assent. It is very easy to utter the words, "Sure I believe God wants to heal me," without bringing every part of your being into alignment with those words. It is very easy to say you believe when you are not required to be accountable to your words, when you are not required to make a complete commitment of body, soul, and spirit to your words. Your body in grave danger from a deadly disease is a good time to consider making such a commitment of belief. You may not have a whole lot to lose if you take a radical step of faith and believe for a divine healing—so why not test your beliefs by taking a stand on God's promises? Mere human words can be very cheap in the society we live in today. Coming into agreement with God's Word is always priceless and true. To receive total healing in any area (mental, emotional or physical) where you have struggled for a long time will require that you bring every part of your being into a unified stand of faith. Binding and loosing prayers will help you come to a point of making a choice to put some feet under your faith.

Coming Into Agreement With God

Sickness and disease can originate in your body from physical causes, particularly if you have open doors of access in your soul for unwelcome organisms to infiltrate. Sickness and disease generally remain in your body because of wrong input, negative words, wrong understanding, and all the things in your soul that are blocking God's healing from coming through your spirit.

Your body is a follower. It is going to trot right along behind whatever seems to be most in control of your belief systems, whether that is your soul or your spirit. It has been scientifically proven that the body has the ability to alter its own chemical structure to come into alignment with intellectually and emotionally powerful negative beliefs (which are recorded and stored in the soul). It has been proven by the medical experts when people have a life-long fear of getting a specific disease, there is a good chance they will. There is also a strong chance that they may die of that same disease if they don't break themselves out of the deception of what they have believed.

But there is also a good side to this incredible potential of your body to realign itself to the most powerful beliefs resident within you. Your faith in the Word of God can help you even out the scales and turn your body's attention to the promises of God in your spirit. If emotionally and intellectually negative thoughts and wrong ideas about your physical health are in control of your belief systems, loose those wrong thoughts and ideas. When you do that, your body will begin to turn its focus around 180 degrees <u>if you have fed and nurtured your spirit with the good promises of God</u>. There must be godly truth and promises in your spirit for your body to believe your spirit is actually in control of your belief systems.

It is your spirit that believes the Word of God. Your spirit believes that God wants to heal all infirmity and disease. When its beliefs outweigh and overshadow the negative beliefs in your soul, your body will begin to realign its chemical structure in agreement with the spirit's beliefs. Haven't you heard of doctors who say, "He's just lost his will to live. If he just believed he could make it, he would. If he doesn't, he will die."

Creating Room To Receive

I have prayed with many Christians who have been given death sentences by doctors. They have been told that there is nothing that can be done for them. Many of these people have seemed to remain alive because of the many prayers others have prayed for them. They are still alive, but they are not getting healed. They are holding on to their faith in God's ability to heal, growing weaker and weaker.

One such Christian told me of how authority figures had spoken into his life since he was a small child, constantly reinforcing fears, negativity, and wrong agreements that he would never live a normal life. He told me that he had always believed that he'd die young. When he told me this, I didn't rebuke his words, I didn't quote power Scriptures to him, and I didn't try to cast a "spirit of death" or whatever out of him. I just asked him why he believed this. He related three authoritative sources of negative input that had fed into his soul throughout his entire life. This caused him to acquire incredibly strong, negative emotional and intellectual beliefs in his soul while still relatively young and impressionable. Now, years later, these beliefs were seemingly entrenched in his soul, firmly blocking a divine healing.

Many ill people have no idea that they are so filled with the effects and influences of wrong agreements entered into because of the negative words of others spoken about their health. To try and recreate this in a comparative visual, picture the lifelong negative input on health issues in an individual's soul as weighing 400 pounds. Picture the positive, godly input in the same individual's spirit as weighing 40 pounds. The body, when in physical distress, will respond to whichever other part of your tripartite being (body, soul, spirit) that seems to be in charge of your belief systems. It is not difficult to determine which entity the body will believe carries the most influence on the belief system— the soul (400 pounds of negative input) or the spirit (40 pounds of good godly input)

So Let's Get Started

The beginning of the healing process can be cooperated with by loosing wrong agreements and wrong diagnoses out of your soul. If your soul's databanks are full of the word curses, impressions and influences of an entire lifetime of doctors, family members, and others speaking negative medical "facts" into it—there is no room for God's input. Such a soul has been so overwhelmed by the incredible weight of such hopeless things, there is no place for God's answer to be received and manifested to the body. The healing power comes first through the individual's spirit, is received in the soul, and then manifests itself to the physical body. When the soul is too clogged with negative input to receive the healing coming through the spirit, it is like arriving at an airport to find out that your gate is all clogged up with passengers and baggage which prevents you from boarding your airplane.

When I am ministering to someone who is sick, I have them pray and I agree with their words. I will lead them in the things they should say, but they pray the prayers. I agree with them. I ask them to repent, reject, and renounce everything they can think of that has been hindering their healing from God. I ask them to cut, sever, break, and destroy the effects and influences of every wrong agreement they have ever entered into, as well as any soul ties that might have been formed through the wrong agreements (see following chapter on Soul Ties). I even have them renounce things that might not even be a factor, but they renounce them anyway.

I have them loose wrong diagnoses from themselves when there is a serious illness that has been tested and confirmed by medical experts. I believe that the doctors may well have the x-rays and tests to support such natural diagnoses, but every diagnosis that does not line up with God's will for a believer's life and Kingdom destiny here on earth is a wrong diagnosis for a Christian to come into agreement with. This type of prayer is divine redirection of the facts from the natural realm into the supernatural realm.

Never Use Your Health As An Excuse

There is an interesting side issue to all of this that I want to cover here, having already covered it in *Breaking the Power*. Your soul will use old word curses and wrong beliefs about your health as an escape mechanism in order to avoid dealing with something it doesn't believe it can or doesn't want to handle. When you learn that such an evasive action will work while you are young, your soul will adapt it to work when you're older. You will just choose different circumstances to apply it to. This is a learned pattern of behavior that is directly related to psychosomatic illnesses.

I have a friend who was invited to attend a conference with several other people and said yes. We've all thought that perhaps we would like to do something in the future that sounds fun, but when it comes right down to actually following through with it, we change our minds. This friend did not want to go to this conference after all, but didn't know how to get out of it. I said, "Why don't you just say you don't want to go?" My friend said that she didn't want to hurt the other peoples' feelings, and they were expecting her to share expenses. So I said, "Then go." My friend said she didn't want to go. "Then tell them so." And we were back to the not wanting to hurt their feelings yada, yada, yada.

Then my friend said, "I just wish my blood pressure would go up, then the doctor would tell me I couldn't travel. There wouldn't be anything I could do about it." Your soul is always looking for a way to enable it to do what it wants or doesn't want to do, without being accountable for any unpleasant side issues. It knows that illness is a good excuse for expecting people to not hold you accountable to fulfill your promises that you no longer want to keep. Your soul can find 100 ways to justify doing something it wants to do, and it can find 100 ways to justify not doing something it doesn't want to do. Yes, her blood pressure shot up and the doctor did forbid her to travel. She had her "out." But this is a dangerous game to play.

When you don't know how to successfully produce answers and results to alleviate the stress and pressure of your life, your soul will invent escape routes by making your body sick. This also applies to developing "headaches" to avoid marital responsibilities. A physical illness means that you don't have to be accountable to resolve that which you are not sure you can or don't want to resolve.

I recently spoke with a very sincere man at a conference I did. He had been to a couple of other conferences and had originally asked for prayer for healing of his back. At the original conference, I told him to pray the prayers in *Shattering Your Strongholds* until the final meeting and be prepared to receive the last teaching on healing. About two hours after the healing meeting, he found me and said, "I am not healed! I am angry at God and I'm angry with you. I am not healed!" I didn't have any problem with the sincerity of his disappointment, and I commended his honesty.

I then asked him to pray after me exactly what I was about to say. Halfway through the prayer, I said something I don't remember asking anyone to pray before, "Though He slay me, I will serve Him." The man broke into deep, body shaking sobs. I said gently, "I think the issue here is: if He doesn't heal you, will you still serve Him?" And I walked away from him, for it was now between him and God. Later he came to me and apologized for blaming me and God for his lack of healing. I told him again it was fine, he had only been honest about what he was feeling.

A few months later, I met him again at another meeting when I returned to the same general area. I noticed deep lines of pain and fatigue etched in his face. I asked, "Are you still mad at me?" He smiled and said no. He was about to sit through the same keys of the Kingdom healing teaching he had sat through before, and I wasn't sure how he was going to react if he wasn't healed again. This particular night, I felt the Lord wanted me to focus particularly on our souls' ability to influence our bodies to become ill. After the meeting, the man came up to me and asked to speak to me privately.

He said, "This is a little embarrassing, but I have to ask you. I've been home for quite a while now because of my back pain, and I don't want to go back to work. I want to go to school instead. If I go back to work, I can't go to school. My brother is on disability because of his bad back, and he isn't planning on ever going back to work. Although I have had many different people pray for me, I've been to the doctors, I've tried almost everything I know, and my back is just getting worse. Do you think my soul is causing my back pain so I have an excuse not to go back to work? Do you think I resent my brother not having to work?"

I replied, "I think God has given you revelation understanding tonight. Are you willing to ask Him to give you all of the details of what is involved in your back pain? Are you willing to let Him do whatever needs to be done to get you ready to serve Him? Are you willing to trust Him for the details of your destiny and your future?"

The man replied, "Yeah, I think I need to do that. Thanks for the straight talk."

At this same meeting, a young woman came up and asked me, "If I have some serious relationship problems with my mother, to the point that I cannot even stand to have her touch me or hug me, do you think these feelings in my soul could be causing the health problems I'm having?"

I replied, "I think God is giving you some revelation understanding tonight. Are you willing to let Him reveal the source of all of the rest of the turmoil in your life?" She said yes.

God's Altar Calls

I rarely lay hands on people and minister to them following meetings any more. When I have finished teaching, I have the people pray a corporate prayer out loud that focuses on the issues I have just taught upon. I believe it is vital that leaders and ministers and teachers stop encouraging people to be so dependent upon their personal ministry after a meeting. While I always spend time to sign books and visit briefly with people after a meeting, I work very hard during that meeting to make them realize that I am a messenger with keys to give them so that they can begin to work with God in every area of their life. It is critical that they understand how to continue cooperating with their heavenly Father after I have gone. I brought them information they needed, and I am no longer important to their spiritual growth or healing.

Montana Ministry

I recently made my first trip to Montana. I taught several sessions at a woman's retreat up in the Beartooth Ridge Mountains (awesome country!) and then returned into Billings where we had public meetings in a large auditorium. I ministered on how to use the keys of the Kingdom to make room to receive healing from God. After ministering healing through corporate prayer with the whole assembly, I went back to sign books at the book table. After about 45 minutes, the last man came through the line in a wheel chair.

His name was Walter and he said that he had come to the meetings because of the incredible difference he had seen in his wife since the woman's retreat a few days earlier. His wife had been deeply depressed for months and had received a wonderful breakthrough at the retreat. Walter told me that he had been in the wheel chair over five years, being completely paralyzed from the waist down. Then he said, "After what has happened in my wife's life, and what I heard tonight about these keys of the Kingdom, I almost believe I can receive my healing from God."

As I signed his book, I felt like my pen went sort of out of control and I wrote, "God bless you, Walter, we'll go for a walk together when I come back to Montana." I am very careful about what I say or do to cause a lamb to be set up for something that may not be in God's timing yet. Or they may not be willing to release all of their accumulated negativity in their soul yet. So, I was a little startled at what I had written. I told Walter to keep praying the binding and loosing prayers from the book, and I would be in agreement with him in prayer even though I would be gone. Two days later, I flew to New Mexico for meetings there.

In New Mexico, I received a phone call from my office. The associate pastor of the church that had hosted my trip to Montana had just called. The men of their church had their men's retreat the weekend after I left and while at the retreat, Walter woke up early on Saturday morning after hearing the words, *"Get up."* He asked if someone had said that to him, but no one had. He heard the words again, *"Get up."* He struggled around in bed and pulled himself to his feet, holding onto the bunk bed. Then he heard, *"Now walk."* Haltingly, he began to walk unsteadily across the room. Within hours, he was running and jumping.

I had not laid hands on Walter, I had not even prayed for him at the meeting. God had met him in the Beartooth Ridge Mountains, one on one, just Walter and God! Walter had begun to cut away the effects and influences of wrong agreements, wrong words, wrong diagnoses, and wrong beliefs in his soul. There was no doubt in Walter's soul that God had performed a miracle healing in his body because he had taken the keys of the Kingdom and used them to open the door of his own prison and walk out. This is why I do not do personal ministry anymore, at least for a season.

I do believe in the power of praying for people, especially in the power of laying on of hands and anointing with oil. But we are entering into a time when I feel it is imperative that people recognize that their faith, the keys of the Kingdom, and God are all that is necessary. I am convinced that I have to keep striving to teach them in such a way that they know that they know that I am there to share information so personal, so practical, so powerful, nothing can withstand their receiving all they need to fulfill their destinies.

Don't Be Loopy

I have long believed that part of the church world today has gotten a little loopy about denying sickness and infirmity. It seems to some that if you admit that you are sick and you do hurt, then something must either be wrong with your faith or with your God. Don't worry about God, He can take care of himself. Have faith in that and have faith in Him. If you hurt and it is a reasonable choice, take a couple of aspirins. Feel better while you begin to pray and talk to Him about the problem.

Don't get under guilt and condemnation about hurting. Don't feel guilty because a cold towel over your forehead would make you feel better. Feeling better while you pray for healing is not a sin. Don't get loopy and don't get rigidly religious. Relax, make yourself a little more comfortable, and pray.

Home Court Advantage

A doctor's bad report, serious x-rays, and negative test results are facts that you don't have to deny. You can step out of the center of the negative natural situation and over onto the positive supernatural promises of God's Word and say, "Yes, doctor, I do see and understand what you're telling me. I see that x-ray and those test results, and I surely do trust your ability to diagnose me in the natural. But you see, I have a supernatural God and I am going to now go and ask Him what He and I are going to do with those natural facts. After I get a second opinion from Him, I'll get back to you."

You don't have to deny natural negative facts surrounding you—if they exist, they're there. You just have to say, "Father, I'm binding myself and these natural facts to your will and purposes for my life right now. I don't know how to handle them, so please help me." And then believe that He will fulfill His part in heaven.

People are being told today that they have all kinds of diseases and infections. Those diagnoses don't mean anything to God. What's important to God is that you come out of agreement with diagnoses that don't fit into His destiny plans for you. It is also important to come into alignment body, soul, and spirit with His plans for you. Your healing may have already been sent with a delivery attempt made. If there was no room to receive it, it went down to the corner to the Holy Ghost Mini Storage. I believe that place is full of healings, full of answers, full of blessings. Get ready to receive yours.

Receiving Healing

Father, I bind my body, my soul, and my spirit to your will and purposes. I loose every wrong belief, every negative diagnosis I've accepted as "truth," every faulty natural understanding I have, all conventional wisdom, every word curse, and every half-truth that is helping these symptoms flourish in my body. If I have any doors open in my soul, I loose every and any hindrance and device the enemy is using against my body. I loose—crush, smash, destroy, tear down, and tear up—any and all strongholds and wrong beliefs that I have allowed to create those open doorways.

I loose all effects and influences of any unwelcome organism in my body. I loose the reproductive ability of any unwelcome, unwanted, mutated alien cells in my body. I bind my body to the DNA blueprint that you imprinted on every single cell in my body before I was even born. Those blueprints still exist in every cell in me. If any part of that DNA was not perfect when I was born because my parents were out from under the blood covering, Father, I ask you to recreate the perfect DNA blueprint you knew I'd need today.

My body has the ability to come into alignment with your power and healing, your truth, your Word. I will not allow it to follow the leading of any doubt, fear, or hopelessness that my soul is trying to establish as reality. The reality is that my spirit has all access to your supernatural truth which transcends natural reality. You are my God. I am your child. And I now believe that your love, grace, and mercy and truth are all I need to become a walking supernatural miracle in the natural realm of life. AMEN!

7

Casting Off Soul Power
and Soul Ties

Soul Ties Begin Here

Many broken Christians have cried out to God to bring them mates, satisfying relationships, money, careers, recognition, fame, appreciation, or whatever they believe will fill the emptiness they feel inside themselves. The desperate hope that God will send one or more of these things to stop the vacuum of neediness within them begins to falter when God does not. Frequently this results in the belief that God doesn't love them enough to care. God cares very much, but He knows that what they are asking for will not fill up their emptiness, because He is the only one who can. He will not give what they *think* they need when it will only be a temporary panacea, ultimately creating more desperation.

Unfulfilled, unhappy, unsatisfied Christians often believe they have to fill up the emptiness of their own souls. If you believe that you must do this, you will view others and things around you according to their value to your soul's desperate agenda for fixing itself. If you have extensive unmet needs, you will seek others who will agree with you for what you need. Wrong agreements that invariably result will always set up the potential for soul ties between unsurrendered souls.

There is too little understanding in the body of Christ today about soul power and soul ties and the danger they create for any Christian's relationships with the Lord and with others. Your born again spirit knows the danger. Your unsurrendered soul, however, does not want this known by anyone. Why? Because your soul believes that its "ties" to other human souls offers it the greatest control possible over them and you as well. In the following paragraphs, I will be rephrasing a few excerpts here from *Breaking the Power,* so as not to try to "reinvent the wheel." This will be to establish the beginning foundation for those who may be unfamiliar with soul power and soul ties.

Our Wits and Our Wills

Man's ability to think and then formulate a response or take an action with regard to his sphere of influence comes from his soul. When Adam and Eve lost their ability to spiritually commune with the Spirit of God in the Garden of Eden, they must have been at quite a loss at first as to what the rest of their lives would be like. Their souls decided that someone had to run things and nominated themselves. This has been the pattern of mankind from that day forward—attempting to control his own destiny by his own wits and will—frequently with great harm and destruction to others. Jesus Christ, however, created a new solution. He presented mankind with a divine Overseer for their lives; His sacrificial offering of His own blood created a path back to spiritual communion with the Father again. He did not come to enslave the souls of mankind, rather He came to set them free from their own futile attempts to pursue joy and peace and abundance.

Andrew Murray said about the soul: "In the history of man's creation we read, 'The Lord God formed man of the dust of the ground' and breathed into his nostrils the breath or spirit of life: thus his spirit came from God; and man became a living soul. The spirit quickening the body made man a living soul, a living person with consciousness of himself. . . . Through the body, man, the living soul, stood related to the external world of sense; could influence it, or be influenced by it. Through the spirit he stood related to the spiritual world and the Spirit of God, where he had his origin; and could be the recipient and the minister of its life and power. Standing thus midway between two worlds, belonging to both, the soul had the power of determining itself, of choosing or refusing the objects by which it was surrounded, and to which it stood related." (Andrew Murray, *The Spirit of Christ*).

I think this is one of the best (if slightly convoluted in structure) descriptions of the human soul. The human soul has an awesome potential for natural power, power that must be surrendered to the higher power of the Spirit of God. Whenever a human soul asserts itself (devoid of any divine influence) as preeminent, other lives are always impacted and God's Kingdom purposes are never given priority consideration. Satan has a definite agenda of wanting to tap into a human soul's ability to impact other people. He wants to use the self-centered goals of the unsurrendered soul to sideline Kingdom purposes, by influencing, inflaming, and inciting the will, intellect, and emotions wherever possible. Satan has always initiated his works of darkness through the souls of men and women.

Watchman Nee says this about the soul, "The greatest advantage in knowing the difference between spirit and soul is in perceiving the latent power of the soul and in understanding its falsification of the power of the Holy Spirit." Right on, Watchman!

God Downsized the Soul's Original Portfolio

After Adam's and Eve's spirits suffered separation from the Spirit of God, I believe God diminished their ability to draw upon the power of their own souls. Without an open spiritual link to communicate with them after their sin, there were no safety guards in place against wrong use of their souls' power. I believe God made the human soul's power latent, recessing it deep within the inner part of man's being. The human mind, will, and emotions were still operative, but on a much lower level than before. This would seem to have been done for man's protection from himself.

For the most part, man has not figured out how to tap into but a little of the potential of that latent power. My computer's thesaurus tells me that the word latent means dormant, hidden, immature, and lurking. Lurking is such a great descriptive word, with such graphic imagery coming to mind! It is not difficult to recognize all of these descriptions in the unsurrendered soul's covert as well as overt attempts at control and power takeovers.

Through extremely focused meditation practices designed to reach within the hidden and dormant parts of man's soul, some have gone deeper into looking for this lurking power than others have. Many cults and "religions" exist just to teach this form of introspective rummaging around in the unsurrendered soul's subconscious. Men and women who have rummaged successfully in their own souls' inner depths have caused great destruction and loss of lives through their ability to control others. Jezebel, Hitler, Jim Jones, David Koresh, the leader of the California cult called Heavens' Gates, all knew how to draw upon their souls' latent power to manipulate neediness in others' souls. Satan is more than ready to assist anyone attempting to draw upon the soul's latent power, as any soul power released through man's own efforts will always be used for wrong reasons.

Soul Power Wants To Control—Spiritual Power Wants to Serve

Some time ago, a young minister told me that he was having trouble trying to teach his young wife that he was her head and she needed to go through him for her relationship with God. This incredibly naïve remark began to clarify for me some of the wrong understandings we have about sbmission and authority in marriages, families, churches, and other authority situations of life.

As individuals Christians, male or female, we are all the same to the Father and to Jesus Christ. Galatians 3:26-29 (NKJ) tells us this, *"For you are all sons of God through faith in Christ Jesus* (this is both male and female). *For as many of you as were baptized into*

Christ have put on Christ. There is neither Jew nor Greek, there is neither slave nor free, there is neither male nor female; for you are all one in Christ Jesus. And if you are Christ's, then you are Abraham's seed, and heirs according to the promise." Christ is our spiritual head, our spiritual covering, and He sees us all equally as beloved children of His Father.

I happen to come from a background of ancestors who were Scottish, Irish, English, German-Dutch, and Cherokee Indian. So, what I am about to say is "politically" correct for a part American Indian to say. Everyone in my entire family is a chief. There are no Indians, we are all full-war bonneted, lance packing chiefs guarding our own turfs. This has been a hard attitude for me to break to become a servant for Christ. I had quite a bit of struggle with the notion that I needed to be in submission to anybody. Submission to authority, I don't think so! That not only contributed to many difficult relationships with my family members, it also contributed greatly to my broken marriage to my childrens' father. And it was a major factor in my early years of struggle with the male heirarchy of the church world and the ministry. But, my dear brothers (open apology here, pass it on), I found much cause to do battle with my sisters as well, so please don't take it personally. Forgive me for the grief I probably caused you.

After years of seeing the raucous unilateral standoffs in my all adult family, no one willing to concede ground to anyone else, I began to finally recognize that someone needed to make decisions even if we traded off every week. The person who is in control bears a certain amount of responsibility for the outcome and consequences of any overall decisions. This brought some interesting reverse psychology reactions from various members of my family as they began to realize the scapegoat potentials here. We may be a bunch of rascals sometimes, but they are my rascals, and I love them.

Some semblance of authority and submission are required in all horizontal relationships in society or chaos will reign. Think of busy intersections during commuter traffic. What if no one submitted to red lights, turn lanes, or any of the laws and rules of the road? When driving, we all need to know who has the right to go and stop and turn and when. What about the lines in grocery stores and in banks? There has to be some rules where the one at the head of the line gets to go next, and the others wait their turn. This requires submission to others who are standing in line in front of you, or people can get ugly.

Authority and Submission in the Marriage

Moving on to a less popular ground where someone has to be at the head of the line, let's consider the marriage relationship. God has said the woman is a helpmeet to the man. I don't know why God chose the structure of authority in the marriage as He did, but it is not our place to question it. Sometimes important decisions need to be made and supported and God has placed the husband in the position as the final decision maker. The helpmeet wife should be consulted and involved in each step of the decision-making process, fulfilling her role as a balance to the husband's thought processes. This decision-making process can be greatly simplified when a husband and wife are willing to pray together and bind their wills to the will of God and bind their minds to the mind of Christ.

Each one of them should ideally recognize that all decisions must be made according to God's will alone, which actually takes decisions out of the realm of the huband's will as well as the wife's will. No marriage ever needs to be dysfunctional because of a standoff of the husband against a stand of the wife (or vice versa). Standoffs of wills create a type of a house divided against itself, thereby giving the enemy open doors to attack its very foundations. The only way to reach any decision in unity is for each will to submit to the authority of the will of God in every situation. This is a choice in a horizontal line of authority that God will work with.

With regard to parents and children, again someone has to be captain of the Good Ship Lollipop or the entire crew will end up sinking the family ark. How wonderful it would be if children were taught from an early age that God has a choice that is right in every situation, and that choice is always in alignment with His overall will for everyone's lives. No one but God can understand how any given choice will hinder or further the spiritual growth of every person involved. That is why God needs to make the choices and why fathers and mothers and children all need to learn to snug their wills up close and personal with His will to get in alignment with Him. This is a choice in a horizontal line of authority that God will work with.

With regard to spiritual leaders and followers, someone needs to be responsible for making the rules of churches and ministries. Hopefully the people who are responsible do have the experience and maturity to know that they must work to get the mind of the Father regarding any of their decisions—especially the far-reaching effects of the decisions they make for a church.

Peterson's *The Message* (1 Timothy 3:3-8) tells us this about leaders in the church: *"If anyone wants to provide leadership in the church, good! But there are preconditions. . . . He must handle his own affairs well . . . for if someone is unable to handle his own affairs, how can he take care of God's church? He must not be a new believer, lest the position go to his head and the Devil trip him up."*

If there were no leaders in church, think of the confusion that could reign in every service. One might be singing, one might be prophesying, another might be asking for an offering, while yet another would be trying to preach. Paul told the Corinthian Christians with regards to their church meetings (1 Corinthians 14:40, KJV), *"Let all things be done decently and in order."* However, this authority is always a horizontal line of authority for the purposes of maintaining order within the body. The vertical line of authority for each member of body comes from Christ himself who sees each believer as unique yet of equal importance. Any time church leaders try to place themselves above an individual believer in respect to the vertical line of relationship with Christ, someone is very, very wrong. There is a serious attempt being made to bring believers into wrong agreements with the leaders to control aspects of the believers' lives.

Inappropriate Role Casting

You have a responsibility to the leaders of your church as well as they have to you. Do not try to put your leaders into roles they are not supposed to fulfill. Do not fall into the trap of flattering and "needing" your leaders' input in order to make them feel important.

There are times when we enter into wrong agreements with people in positions of authority because we seek their approval and hope to set up their potential assistance for our own goals. It is a dangerous and dreadful thing to try to mix justifying our own soulish needs and desires with God's purposes for His spiritual leaders.

Whenever a husband (or a wife) attempts to place himself (or herself) in a position of authority between the other partner and his or her vertical relationship to Christ, the one attempting to do so is operating out of the soul. If any emotions are revving up, if the will is digging in, if the mind is tumbling around with sarcasm and accusations, the soul is about to start a parade. Soul power is being exerted and wrong agreements are either in the offing, or a major soul war is brewing. This is a good time to begin binding your will and the will of your spouse to the will of God, as well as both your minds to the mind of Christ.

With regard to the parent/child relationship while children are still in the home and hopefully learning about God, the parent should be binding his or her own will to God's will in every decision and direction given to a son or daughter. Parents should also be binding the wills and the minds of their children to God's will and Christ's mind. The motivation of decisions made and directions given by the parents will be judged by God. The question to be answered will be: was the parent's motivation behind any decision or action to turn the child towards learning the will of God or simply to control the child's behavior, irregardless of how wrong that behavior might have been?

Who Really Gets the Glory?

Soul power was never intended to further any part of the family structure, the work of the Church, or the Kingdom purposes of God. Yet there are some extremely powerful and charismatic Christian ministers operating out of the power of their own unsurrendered souls who believe they have God's purposes at heart. However, the benefit they derive for themselves (recognition, fame, money, power, influence) is almost guaranteed to be the hidden agenda of their souls. Whatever soulish accomplishments come forth initially will eventually deteriorate into humanistic, immoral, or controlling efforts unless the individual has a real face-to-face confrontation with God himself—up close and personal! I remember one minister asking me what I thought about a meeting we had just been in with an extremely charismatic and high-energy, power-Christian evangelist. I cautiously replied, "I think he was quite impressive, perhaps operating a little too much in the soulish realm."

The other minister looked at me with surprise and said, "Liberty, if we didn't all operate a little bit in the soulish realm, we'd never get anything done for God." I shivered at those words, for I knew that this declaration made perfect sense to not only this minister, but to far too many other spiritual leaders today, as well. The unsurrendered soul's agendas are never for God's ultimate glory, they are always geared to receiving personal glory—while throwing a few bones God's way.

But I Need To Know I'm Appreciated

It is extremely important to reach a point where you stop trying to get affirmation and approval from

171

the imperfect people in your life. That's a hard one for almost everyone. I know people 70 years old and older who still say, "You know, my father never approved of me. My mother never affirmed me." It is very tragic that the effects and influences of past betrayals, old hurts, and unmet needs are still so painful in their lives in the present. If you need approval and affirmation from the imperfect people in your life, it puts you in a position where you will forever be influenced by whether or not you get that approval and affirmation.

We could, however, all learn something from some of the criticisms and/or suggestions other people make with regard to us. Unfortunately, many just try to sluff them off, while burying their vulnerabilities even deeper. I am always impressed when I see people who can consider even their worst enemy's remarks as a flag to mark an area they want to take to God in prayer. I believe God may actually trigger some of the painful remarks by others to get our attention when we have not listened to repeated warnings of the Holy Ghost about unhealed areas of our souls that make us vulnerable to human influence. God will use whatever means He has to when He needs to challenge our carefully constructed denial mechanisms. He wants us to acknowledge these areas exist, voluntarily bring them to Him, and then trust Him to fix them. I think God considers all tidy "I'm just fine, thank you" facades in unsurrendered souls as items for His priority exposure list.

Satan cannot read your mind, but he has no problem bringing people across your path who will cause you to react to their pushing on your unmet needs and unhealed hurts. He knows everything that has ever happened to you, and all he has to do is judge your reactions to his recreating your worst experiences to see whether or not you are healed in a given area. If you do not react to the pressure he brings, he will mark a former experience off as a dead link. Then he will seek another area to pressure you about, a hot spot of your soul, a live link so to speak. If you are not healed in that area, which he easily judges by your reaction to another person's criticism or pressure, then he will try to crush you there.

Who Have You Been Agreeing With?

Your soul is interested in trying to involve you with people who are like you, who know your pain and understand why you are the way you are. Your spirit always seems to be pushing you towards taking risks to be who God knows you should be. The soul finds that extremely discomforting. If you are protecting deep unmet needs and unhealed hurts in your soul, particularly of years of great standing, the very best thing you can have is somebody who will speak truth and grace into those issues. Someone who will pressure you a little bit in love.

Philippians 2:1-4 *(The Message)* tells us Paul said this, *"If you've gotten anything at all out of following Christ, if His love has made any difference in your life, if being in a community of the Spirit means anything to you, if you have a heart, if you care—then do me a favor. Agree with each other, love each other, be deep-spirited friends. Don't push your way to the front; don't sweet-talk your way to the top. Put yourself aside and help others get ahead. Don't be obsessed with getting your own advantage. Forget yourselves long enough to lend a helping hand."* What an agenda-free description of healthy friendship and fellowship! No soul tie set ups here.

Exactly what is a soul tie? I teach about them. I pray with people to break them. I recognize them. I've been involved in some in times past. But as of yet, I still do not have a one-line definition for them. Soul ties happen when you enter into a wrong agreement with another person, wrong agreements ranging all the way from soulish prayers prayed together to agreements to commit fornication and violent crime.

I'm unsure where soul ties "operate," perhaps somewhere in between the natural realm and the spiritual realm. I don't know if it is important to know, perhaps it is. The issue I address is that you need to break them and the keys of the Kingdom will effectively do that. There are times when you are in a crisis and you need to just get out of it. Self-examination of the reasons for the crisis can come later, and hopefully you will learn to avoid the crisis again. If you are in a house on a cliff and an earthquake starts, the logical course of action is run for your life—away from the cliff. It is not to go the bookshelf or get on the internet to learn about earthquakes. Hello? You can do that later if you manage to get out alive.

We don't always remember our priorities in a crisis. I will never forget seeing a poster of a very harried looking person flailing around in a swamp, with the caption over his head: *It is hard to remember—when you're up to your neck in alligators—that your original orders were to drain the swamp.*

How Can You Tell If A Soul Tie Has Been Formed?

Christians can enter into some wrong agreements (the origin of souls ties) ignorantly, but there will always be some kind of check in their spirits from the Holy Spirit. The check might be just a small sensing of uneasiness that something is not right, but not knowing what to do about it. I believe the Holy Spirit always tries to warn a Christian if there is a real lack of understanding of the serious consequences of an impending action. But when we choose not to heed warning signs in our spirits, it is because our souls have so much control in our lives. Your spirit always hears what God is saying, but your soul can block out any further transmission. Sometimes, when irreversible danger is inevitable if you go any further, God may have to and will send a powerful message that even your soul can't block.

He has done that several times in my life. These power messages can be quite painful and abrupt if all other spiritual input has been ignored. I have been motivated to hear His little communiques as quickly as I can. One such message came, before I was ever saved, in the form of a read-end collison involving the sitting-still-rear end of my Pontiac and the fast-moving-front end of a large moving van. That rear end collision (okay, God, I'm listening) forced me to leave a job that I needed to be out of quickly. I had sensed several little "twinges" that there was something wrong in the training center where I was working, but I ignored them because it was a good sales job and the "stated" purpose of the center seemed good. God knew that for me to remain involved with this group of people, even in an independent contractor status as a sales person, could have ultimately involved me in a group sweep of official action against the leadership of the center. He "rear ended" me out of there just in time when I wouldn't listen to His more low-key warnings.

Usually God will let you go through hard consequences that boil up out of wrong agreements. However, when there are life-threatening dangers involved in the consequences, He may well set up circumstances to knock you out of them. There are many things Christians have erroneously viewed as acts of the devil that have been God's stop gaps in a downward slide of dangerous consequences. God will use hard things on hard heads to save them from hard fates when He has to.

The soul will often attempt to block out all warnings from God, family members, and friends if it perceives a benefit awaiting it. How many times have you known a family member, who would not listen to any counsel or advice, to enter into a difficult marriage that later ended up in a painfully messy divorce? How many times have you known a friend, who would not listen to any counsel or advice, to enter into a wrong agreement to buy an expensive car, a big house, or a business that ends up in great loss? Any wrong agreement the soul insists upon making always holds forth some kind of perceived benefit that often overshadows common sense, good advice, and logical reasoning.

Not All Prayer is Good Prayer

Most worldly agreements are fairly obvious to Christians. They are still made at times, but great rationalizing, justifying, and denial are involved in doing so. As stated in previous chapters, these are the building blocks of soulish strongholds built to keep all godly advice and truth at bay. One wrong agreement that is not as obvious to the Christian is the wrong agreement in soulish prayers. Not all prayer is good prayer. Pure prayer is, *"Not my will regarding any part of this, God, but thy will alone be done."* Binding and loosing prayer principles are very helpful in clearing the deck so you can get to this purest prayer.

Wrong agreements occur whenever you seek out others to pray soulish prayers with you:

1. To garner personal agreement on a soulish stand you are making.

2. To get others to take sides with your soulish viewpoints.

3. To gather support for a soulish action you do not know how to push through on your own.

This happens a lot with our "favored" prayer partners, the ones we trust with words that should never be said in the first place. These are usually people who understand us, who think like us, and who will never speak blunt truth to us. Lord, give us prayer partners who will jerk us up short every time we think about praying wrong. The greatest way to pass gossip in the church world, without seeming to be gossiping, is through a prayer line or with a prayer partner. "Well, I am only telling you this so you'll pray, but have you heard what's going on in Betty Jean's life? Remember now, I am only telling you this so you'll know how to pray effectively." If you believe that line, I have a bridge over the San Francisco Bay I'd like to sell you!

I have often heard people wanting others to agree with them, with only the "best" of intentions (of course), for the removal of a pastor. They can be so self-anointed and self-righteous about their good intent for their church. That is wrong. God brings the pastors and God removes the pastors. Any Christian who thinks it is right to get with others and agree for the removal of a leader is deceived. They set themselves up for a possibility of soul ties with the others they agree with. They should be speaking right agreement over their leadership, not wrong agreement, agreement like this:

Lord, I thank you for every single leader you have placed in our church. I ask you to give them inspiration, I ask that you stir up their anointing, and I ask that you bless them and cover them with grace and mercy. I bind them to your purposes, that they will walk in the center of your will for our church and that heavenly things will be accomplished on earth. I bind their minds to the mind of Christ, and I ask that you give them new understanding of your truth, that you pour out your wisdom upon them. I choose to believe that they will embrace your will and your truth and walk in their earthly destinies with great strength and power. I bind every person in our church, including myself, to your will for our lives. Teach us how to be more humble and aware of our own wicked ways, always seeking your face and speaking forth right agreement concerning your will for every person we know. Teach us how to break the power of all wrong agreements that have ever been spoken about this church and its leaders, teach us how to always pray in agreement with your Word and your will for our leaders.

God always moves with power in response to right agreements spoken, and the enemy always moves in response to wrong agreements spoken—especially those spoken in self-righteous, soulish prayers.

Here are a few more examples of soulish prayers of wrong agreements. How many times I have had people ask me to agree that, in the name of Jesus (of course), they will get to marry Judy or Betty or John or Jerry. I will never agree with them on that prayer. But I will pray with them and bind their wills, as well as Judy's and/or Jerry's wills (etc.) to the will of God. I will loose the effects and influences of all wrong prayers, all wrong agreements, and soul tie issues from everyone involved. I have had many other people tell me something like, "We just love that young man over there, he's so sweet and so spiritual. We just know that he ought to be married to that young woman over there. So we get together every Thursday night and pray that they recognize that God wants the two of them to get married." Good grief, they don't know any such thing!

God is the only one who knows the destiny purpose of that young man and that young woman. Do I think you can actually pray a self-targeted couple into a wrong marriage agreement? Not directly, but you could begin to influence them to enter into wrong agreements with you if you are persuasive enough.

Smells Good

You can be praying for all kinds of things that look good to you but have nothing to do with God's plans and purposes. Soulish prayers usually sound good, smell good, and always promise some kind of a benefit to you—and you are always sure that you know exactly how God wants to answer them. What would be the benefit to your soul in praying soulish prayers for the young man and the young woman above? You could forever say with great spirituality, "I used to pray every Thursday for them to get married. I'm so glad that God answered my prayers and put them together." Then when their marriage begins to go sour, you suddenly feel they have let your prayer reputation down. So you go and find another couple to pray into wedded bliss. If you have been involved in praying for someone to marry another person and their marriage hits the rocks, I believe you really have an obligation to begin to pray right prayers for them every day, every hour if necessary! Right prayers are the prayers that they will both surrender to the will of God, so His will can be done in their lives.

People who pray soulish prayers often put out information that they have spent a lot of time praying for good things that happen. Have you noticed how no one goes around repeatedly saying how much they have prayed for things that haven't happened? Their words usually sound like this, "Oh, yes, I was thrilled to see that such and such finally happened. I've been praying for that to happen for ever so long." (I love what I once heard Iverna Tompkins say about that: "Who cares?") Don't you think their souls get religious satisfaction from saying how much they have prayed for this or that, while subliminally hinting, "Don't you want me to pray for you, too? You see, I do have a proven track record in getting my prayers answered."

We should always be ready to pray for others, always! But we should be far more reticent in our motives for telling others how much we pray for them, unless they are asking for such an assurance. Otherwise, we should be far more interested in praying anonymously. I have a group of intercessors who pray every Tuesday night in my office or in my home. I have cautioned all of them to keep to themselves what we are praying about and who we are praying for—especially after answers come. God needs to get the glory for the answered prayers, not those who have prayed.

No Such Thing As a Good Soul Tie

There is *no* such thing as a good soul tie. Not with a prayer partner, not with a spiritual leader, not with a spouse, not with our children. Whenever you are involved in a soul tie with someone, that other person is your first choice of agreement on issues, and God comes second or maybe even third or fourth. You are called to be one in flesh when you are married and believers are all called to be one in spirit. There is nowhere in the Bible where it says any of us are to be one in soul or be soul mates with anybody.

I believe there are a large number of Christian parents who have unhealthy soul ties to their sons and daughters. We all know Christian parents who seem to function very well in their own spiritual walks until something happens in the lives of their children. Of course I believe we should care deeply about our children and how their lives are going. But if their lives are going badly because of wrong decisions they are making, they often are experiencing the consequences of their choices. How wonderful it is when a parent/child relationship has been built in such a fashion that a growing or grown son or daughter will listen to and heed godly counsel from their parents. But if the grown son or daughter won't listen to godly counsel, then the parent's only recourse is to talk to God about the situation in prayer—He will always listen.

A parent's prayer should be a prayer of faith that God cares more than the praying parent does. Parents need to realize that the concern they have over need in their child's life is tiny compared with the multiplied-million-times-over love and concern that God has for the same child. In the original Greek manuscripts of the New Testament, the word faith often comes back to this simple yet perfect definition: confidence and trust in the goodness of God. Family members and finances seem to be the hardest areas for Christians to have all-inclusive confidence and trust that God is doing everything necessary.

I love my three children and my daughter-in-law and grandson very much. I believe I would stand toe-to-toe in hand-to-hand combat with a bear to protect one or all of them in the natural. I pray for them every day for protection in the spiritual realm. I am sincerely concerned about their spiritual, soulish, and physical welfare. Yet there is no great heart-stopping fear in me when they seem to be following the roads of wrong choices. I wish they wouldn't, but they are all quite stubborn and strong willed (I have no idea where they got that!). So I bind them to God's will and purposes and loose the effects and influences from them of stronghold thinking and wrong agreements. I ask God to cover them with grace and mercy and teach them what He must.

One day I said to one of my friends, "I feel sort of guilty that I'm not more worried about some of the trips my kids seem to still be taking around Mt. Sinai in pursuit of their own ways. I believe God is answering my daily prayers for them, but do you think I should be more concerned about their mistakes and wrong choices?"

My dear friend said, "No, I think it is great that you pray and then are able to leave them in God's hands the rest of the day and get on with your other assignments for Him. You are at a place where you really do trust God to bring them all the way in, aren't you?"

Parent/Child Soul Ties

One Christian mother I know (in another state) has a son who is in and out of jail, in and out of drug addiction, in and out of all kinds of things. Every time he gets into serious consequences, he pulls on the soul tie between her and himself, and she runs and rescues him. The wrong agreement involved here is probably that her son needs her more than he needs anyone else (her part) and that his mother will always save him (his part). She has unmet needs to be important and valuable to others, especially her offspring, and he is smart enough to use those needs to enable him to continue to pursue his own soul's wrong beliefs.

This mother once said to me, "I just don't understand why God lets Frank do these things. When everything is all right in Frank's life, my faith is just fine. When Frank is in trouble, it tears my faith apart. Why doesn't God see that!" I was actually speechless at this illogical diatribe, and those of you who have heard me teach know this is not an easy state to accomplish in me!

I asked her to consider that she had a soul tie with her son that was actually enabling his behavior. She has a very hard time believing that her great "love" for her son has been helping him to stay on the unhealthy way he had chosen. I managed to convince her to pray binding and loosing prayers to break those soul ties a couple of times. But soul-tie breaking is not always a one-time breaking, especially when the other person is so dependent upon your responding to the pull of that soul tie. If you are involved in a soul tie and you break it, the other person will attempt to reattach it. If you still want it, you will respond and come back into wrong agreement with this person. It is a quite amazing thing how soon the other person will make contact after a prayer to break a soul tie, asking if everything is all right. I have found that it usually happens within twenty-four hours, and it always comes in the guise of great concern for the one who has just broken the soul tie. The other person knows he or she has lost something, they are just not sure what.

After one teaching I gave on the danger of soul ties, I was contacted a week later by the pastor of that church. This pastor said, "Several people have prayed and broken soul ties with people out of their pasts, and it is incredible how many people have surfaced out of their pasts wanting to know if they were all right. Some by mail, some by phone, and one even turned up out of the past in person the morning after your teaching!"

Husband/Wives Soul Ties

I counsel husbands and wives to pray and break soul ties between each other as these horizontal ties get in the way of a strong, healthy vertical relationship with God. Everyone today enters into marriage with unmet needs, unhealed hurts, and unresolved issues. These can create a crushing set of expectations for another human being to try to fulfill. Quoting from *Breaking the Power,* I feel it would be expedient to reiterate the following: The love in a perfect union in marriage before God must come from the spirits of a man and a woman. Love that comes out of godly, spiritual unity never grows bored or disappointed or cold when time passes and circumstances change. Love based in spiritual unity continues to see the gift in the other person when the gift wrapping begins to fray and wrinkle. The soul and the body express marital love, but **the spiritual union between the husband and wife is the only thing that can be counted on to never change**.

A soul tie between a husband and wife comes from a mutual agreement that the other partner is first in line for the meeting of all needs, whether reasonable or otherwise. There are certain needs in wounded souls that no human being can ever meet. A meeting of some needs will certainly be accomplished in a marriage, for each partner is a gift to the other partner. But ties between the souls of the two partners cause a man and a woman to look to each other for assurance, healing, support, sustenance, answers, and guidance before they look to God. When one partner's dependency upon the other partner is excessively out of balance, it may seem flattering at first. But eventually this intense neediness begins to drain the partner who is always expected to meet the needs of the other partner. It is an issue of an unfulfilled soulish need and unrealized expectations in a man or woman that prompts the words, "I don't love you anymore." These words come from an unsurrendered soul's bitterness and resentment that its expectations and needs have not been fulfilled and met.

How Do You Avoid Soul Ties?

First of all, you need to realize why you would seek them—they come from a wrong agreement that you will get some benefit from another person to compensate for the unmet needs, unhealed hurts, and unresolved issues of your soul. The best insurance against wrong agreements and resulting ties is to pray the binding and loosing prayers to make a way for God to get into these areas and heal you. Nothing and no one but Him will ever fill up the emptiness within you. Begin to be aware of your desire to have others come into agreement with your personal opinions, or others seeking your agreement with their personal opinions. Be aware of your desire or others' desires to agree on emotional judgments. Beware of wanting to pray in agreement only with believers who think "just like you do." We've all avoided praying with people who might tell us we're being soulish.

The following is a condensed, newly revised version of the breaking of soul ties prayer in *Breaking the Power:*

Training-Wheel Prayer for Breaking Soul Ties

Lord, I have been looking to others to fix the need and the pain inside of me. I have made wrong agreements, and I have allowed relationships with other people to get out of alignment with your will for me. Forgive me for having sought life-changing satisfaction and fulfillment from anyone other than you. I now loose, cut, and sever any and all wrong agreements and resulting soul ties I have willingly or ignorantly entered into. I break apart, shatter, dissolve, and reject these soul ties and every soulish satisfaction they have provided for me.

I am choosing to bring my needs and vulnerabilities to you alone. I will remember that fear is but an emotional reaction to the unresolved issues I have never allowed you to reach into. I will tear down my self-defense systems and let you come into the deepest part of my hidden pain. I've tried too long and too unsuccessfully to get my own human expectations fulfilled. Increase my awareness of the attempts of my unsurrendered soul to get its expectations met, and help me to act immediately whenever I sense it trying to do it again. Increase my awareness of old patterns of behavior I need to loose. Increase my awareness of wrong thinking I need to loose and reject. Increase my awareness that I can trust you with everything I let you get close to. Help me to recognize every high thing I've allowed my soul to put up between me and you, and I WILL PULL THEM ALL DOWN. In Jesus' name, Amen.

8

Agreement Releases Power

Christians in Wrong Agreeements?

On my web site, I receive so many questions and prayer requests that say: "I have been told that I have a curse on my life. I believe it is several generational curses. I am a firm believer in God and Jesus Christ, and I am in prayer every day; yet I am poor, sick, and fearful. I have done some background research on my family history and I have found . . . . How do I break these generational bondages?"

My response is generally like this: "You have come into a wrong agreement with someone regarding this belief that you have a curse on your life. This allows another person as well as spirits to manipulate your beliefs and ideas. Proverbs 26:2 tells us, *'Like a flitting sparrow, like a flying swallow, a curse without cause shall not alight'* (NKJ). If you are born again, washed in Christ's blood, you have been forgiven for past sins, even the sins of your fathers. Generational bondage is generally generational wrong thought patterns and wrong attitudes acquired from repeated family exposure. They cannot be conferred like curses upon a Christian unless the Christian gives them a place to land by coming into agreement with them. Loose any wrong agreements that you can be cursed from past generational sins, and agree with your status as a new creature, a child of God. Wrong agreement brings forth the power of darkness and bondage. Right agreement brings forth God's power and freedom."

Many of the questions I respond to and the majority of the prayer requests we receive involve wrong agreements. I am hopeful that the following paragraphs will help others begin to recognize the damage of accepting and entering into wrong agreements.

Beware of False Prophecy

I have been concerned about the mixture of soul and spirit in the flood of prophecies in the body of Christ during the last two decades. I struggle with so many of the "feel-good" prophecies being given, probably with all good intentions on the part of the one prophesying. These prophecies sound very much like the prophecies Jeremiah complained about to God, *"Ah, Sovereign LORD, the prophets keep telling them, 'You will not see the sword or suffer famine. Indeed, I will give you lasting peace in this place.' Then the LORD said to me, 'The prophets are prophesying lies in my name. I have not sent them or appointed them or spoken to them. They are prophesying to you false visions, divinations, idolatries and the delusions of their own minds"*

(Jeremiah 14:13-14, NIV). Many are prophesying peace and prosperity and safety today.

In searching through the Word of God, I do not see how prophecies that all will be well and good (don't worry—be happy) will ever come to pass in America in these last days of the Church age until God's people begin to fulfill 2 Chronicles 7:14, obeying every phrase in one accord, in right agreement. God spoke to Jeremiah about what will come to pass when a false prophecy is given and others come into agreement with it. Jeremiah 14:15-16 (NIV), *"Therefore, this is what the LORD says about the prophets who are prophesying in my name: I did not send them, yet they are saying, 'No sword or famine will touch this land.' Those same prophets will perish by sword and famine. And the people they are prophesying to will be thrown out into the streets of Jerusalem because of the famine and sword. There will be no one to bury them or their wives, their sons or their daughters. I will pour out on them the calamity they deserve."*

The danger in false prophecy appears to be equally to those who do it and those who blindly accept and agree with it. No one has to come into agreement with a word given by anyone. This was something I had to be taught many years ago after suffering much anguish and fear over false prophetic words given to me by Christians who were older in the Lord. I will never forget when a dear father in the faith said to me, "Liberty, just because someone says it does not mean you have to believe it." Prophecy should never be despised or quenched, but all prophetic words should be prayed about, studied in the Word, and then taken before God for confirmation.

I use the keys of the Kingdom to be sure I am in a right attitude within my own soul when I hear a prophetic word. There are times when our souls have an offense against another person, or a word spoken goes against a favorite belief, or we may be simply feeling cranky. That is when I bind my will to the will of God and bind my mind to the mind of Christ, that my soul will receive or reject the word according to the instructions that will come through my spirit from the Holy Spirit. My soul must be as under submission and clear of prejudice as it can be to hear what the Spirit may be speaking regarding the word being spoken.

I want to be spiritually attuned to whatever thing the Holy Spirit may be doing or speaking, while submitting to and exercising (by reason of use) the Spirit's gift to all believers of the discerning of spirits. This gift of the Spirit is given to the believer for recognizing if a human soul, a wrong spirit, or the Holy Spirit is the source of any prophecy. All prophetic words spoken are not true prophecy from the Holy Spirit. Paul said, *"Do not quench the Spirit; do not despise prophetic utterances. <u>But examine everything carefully</u>; hold fast to that which is good"* (1 Thessalonians 5:19-21, NAS). Examine means to prove something is true.

We must be very careful not to let our unsurrendered souls be the judge of whether something is or is not the Holy Ghost. It is our souls that want us to crane our necks and bob our heads around to see who is giving the prophecy. We must stop judging prophetic words by whether or not we think we can trust the prophesying person's spirituality. The identity of the one prophesying should not be the determining factor in our attempt to examine if the prophecy is of the Holy Ghost. Clearing our own soul of prejudice and preconceived ideas to receive confirmation or instruction given into our spirits by the Holy Spirit should be the determining factor.

We all need to run reality checks on ourselves before we would prophesy as an oracle speaking for Almighty God. I believe some false prophecies are a result of preconceived ideas in a would-be prophet's soul, preconceived ideas looking for a public platform of expression. While this is certainly not to be construed as an attempt to establish a carved-in-stone tenent of the faith, I believe a prophetic word should be somewhat of a surprise to the prophet rather than a validation of what the prophet has been expecting (or even hoping) that God would say all along. One other caution, never judge a corrective prophesy given to someone (by another person or yourself) by the fact that you have always felt that someone needed to correct the person in exactly that way.

I remember once hearing an evangelist say that a well-known minister told him that a television evangelist's fall into sin was no surprise to him. The minister said harshly, "I've been watching him very closely for years, just waiting for this to happen."

The evangelist listened to the minister, expressing genuine shock as he said, "You've suspected this brother was struggling, perhaps even sinking into temptation for years? And all you did was just watch and wait for this to happen? <u>May God judge you</u> for not falling on your face in intercession the first moment you suspected he needed prayer, pleading for God's empowerment in his life that he would overcome."

Fear's Wrong Agreement

Fear is an emotional reaction to the pressure on an unresolved issue (usually unresolved trauma) that Satan brings, when he tries to push your reactions out of line. When you come into agreement with fear, you are disobeying the command of the Scriptures where Jesus said, *"Fear not, little flock; for it is your Father's good pleasure to give you the kingdom"* (Luke 12:32, KJV). In fact, the Bible is full of *fear nots*, both in the Old and the New Testament. Disobeying this oft repeated command means that you open doors of access in your soul for further invasion of your life with the fear tactics of the enemy. God has repeated himself about this issue of fear (which is a powerful negative emotional reaction) all through the Bible. The King James Version translates the original manuscripts to say that the Lord has said <u>fear not</u> at least 47 times in the Old Testament and 15 times in the New Testament.

Fear is not an evil spirit (see next chapter). The answer to great fear is to realize that the fear itself is a symptom of something you desperately need for God to heal and to resolve for you. Praying right prayers, right agreement with others who will pray right prayers, reading the Word, and determining that God needs to be given access into the deepest part of your inner being will help.

Right Prayer

Effective prayer is about learning to pray right prayers so you become an instrument for God's will to be manifested on earth. Do I think that binding and loosing prayers are the only right prayers? Not at all, but I think they will get you to the only right prayer that exists, being: *"Not my will be done, Father, but THY WILL BE DONE!"* Many of us think we know exactly how to pray in most situations. I have learned that there are all kinds of situations where I don't have a clue what to pray. I did one weekend long seminar in a large home a few years ago. An exotically beautiful woman who looked part Black, part Oriental, part Indian, came into that meeting where she spent most of the entire time sitting on the floor in front of me, soaking up everything I said. When I was through, I asked if there was anybody who would like prayer. As everyone in this particular group seemed quite reticient about having anyone hear their prayer needs, we went into another room where I prayed for each one privately.

This woman came into the room when it was her turn for prayer, identifying herself as "Sylvia" (not her real name). She said, "I've only been a Christian for three weeks, and I'm so excited about what you've been teaching. I just love being a Christian, and now I can use the keys of the Kingdom, too. But what I really want you to pray is whether or not Jeff and I should get married. I'm 40 years old and Jeff is 42."

Then she said, "But there is something I should tell you before you pray. I was born a boy. When I was 12 years old, my mother was slowly sliding into mental illness over her devastation that my wealthy father was publicly flaunting many girlfriends all over town. One day my mother said to me, "I do not want you to grow up and become a man like your father. I will put a great deal of money into a bank account for you. I will get you the finest plastic surgery and sex change possible, if you will but do this one thing for me. I want you to become a girl instead of a boy. Will you do this for me?"

195

Here was a 12-year-old boy with a mentally ill mother and a father who had ripped their family to pieces. This boy agreed with his mother's request. The mother arranged for the initial surgery to be performed and then set up and prepaid all future surgeries that would be needed. A trust fund was established for the now teenage girl's future, and shortly thereafter, the mother killed herself. Now nearly thirty years later this woman was asking me if I would pray whether she and Jeff should get married. I have to admit that less than fifteen years earlier, I would probably have said, "Get your 501s, a pair of boots, and come on—we're going to the doctor and get this straightened out." But, bless you, Lord, I've learned a lot in the last 15 years.

I took her hands and I began to pray: *"Sylvia, I bind your will to the will of God. I bind your mind to the mind of Christ that He will reveal to you the very thoughts and purposes in His heart. He's going to talk to you like you've never heard Him speak before. I bind you to the truth of God's mercy and grace and love and healing. I bind your feet to the paths that you've been ordained to walk since before you were conceived in your mother's womb. I bind your hands to the work that God has always ordained for you to do. Father, I loose wrong counsel of man off your child, and I loose all wrong beliefs and wrong ideas out of her soul. I loose the effects and influences of all wrong vows and wrong covenants she has ever made. I loose the effects and influences of all wrong agreements she has ever entered into. Father, fill this child with grace and mercy, unmeasured love and healing. Amen."*

Sylvia threw herself into my arms, sobbing and sobbing. Then she said, "I just love being a Christian, this is so wonderful. But you didn't pray about whether Jeff and I should get married!"

I said, "Right." So, I prayed the same prayer as above for Jeff. I bound his mind to the mind of Christ, his will to the will of God, and his feet to the paths God wanted him to walk. I loosed the effects and influences of any wrong understanding, attitudes, patterns of thinking, and wrong agreements from him. I asked for God's great grace and mercy upon him. Then I prayed that God's will would be done in both their lives. Sylvia was so excited, she danced out of the room fully convinced that God would tell her exactly what to do. I was just as convinced. I didn't have a clue about what God's was going to do with her life. But I knew He did. Man and woman have always been able to get themselves into the most awful of situations. Sometimes willingly, sometimes into things totally out of their control. But we have a God who is not confused or upset by anything that any one of His children have ever gotten themselves or someone else into. He knows how to get them out and bring himself glory in the process!

When I'm on television, I always get phone calls from desperate people: wrong lifestyles, child molesters, spouse abusers, liars, adulterers. Frequently they say, "I'm about ready to kill myself. I love God, but I don't know what to do. I just saw you talk about these principles on television, and there seemed to be a little glimmer of hope for me in your words. Do you think this message can help me?"

I say, "Absolutely."

I have received tragic phone calls from youth pastors and deacons and grandfathers from across the

United States, saying, "I can't go to my pastor, I can't go to my board, I can't go to my family. If they knew, I would lose the only support system I have. But I'm struggling with this. I'm struggling with that. Could these principles help me?"

I say, "Yes, they can, absolutely!"

If they want to tell me details, I gently stop them and say, "It doesn't really matter what the details are. Are you ready to bind your will to the will of God? Are you ready to let God bring His will to pass and trust Him to do the right thing, no matter how it shakes out in your life? Do you want to let go of the effects and influences of everything that has happened and trust Him to know how to work it out?"

I have been reminded by others that many churches teach that women should not counsel men on such personal issues. I think that is a fine rule, thank you very much. Now, all that needs to happen is for God to be able to lead these desperate men to men who can help them understand the underlying sources of their wrong desires and thoughts (unmet needs, unhealed hurts, and unresolved issues in their souls) and teach them how to use the keys of the Kingdom in prayer. This will help these men to open up their wounds to God and allow Him to heal them.

At one point a few years ago, I had several obscene phone calls over a period of several months. One day a man called just as I had finished quite a time of prayer with the Lord. The minute he began his dialogue, I began praying over the top of what he was saying, *"Father, thank you for having this poor man call me. I bind his will to your will that he would be free. I bind his mind to the mind of Christ that he will hear the very thoughts, intents, and purposes within Christ's heart towards him. I bind him to the truth of the grace and mercy and freedom you want to give to him. I loose all influences of the enemy off of him. I loose the wrong beliefs and ideas he has about how to make himself feel better. Heal him of the pain and need that drives him to make these calls. Heal him of the bad memories and of the old fears that tear at his mind and sleep. I loose the layers of lies that have been constructed over his unmet needs, unhealed hurts, and unresolved issues. Lord, I ask you to pour out your love upon him and heal him. Set him free to be all you want him to be. Bless him, Father God, and help him to realize that you love him very much. Amen."* The man was speechless. I could hardly hear him breathing, but I knew he was there. I think the enemy knew he had made a big mistake that day, for I believe I'll see that man in heaven.

The Power of Agreement

Agreement seems to be a law and force of it own, just like gravity. Right agreement results in light and good, wrong agreement results in darkness and evil. If we flirt with the law of gravity by dancing, fighting, or sleeping on the edge of a cliff and we fall off—frantic prayer will not stop us from being smashed into oblivion at the foot of that cliff. We ignored the obvious consequences of the law of gravity. We must not flirt with words of wrong agreement and ignore their consequences. We are better off to be silent than create darkness and evil with our words.

Jesus said in Matthew 12:34-37 (NKJ), *"Out of the abundance of the heart the mouth speaks. A good man out of the good treasure of his heart brings forth* (speaks) *good things, and an evil man out of the evil treasure brings forth* (speaks) *evil things. But I say to you that for every idle word men may speak, they will give account of it in the day of judgment. <u>For by your words you will be justified, and by your words you will be condemned.</u>"*

In Acts 4:3, Peter and John were arrested by the temple officials and Sadducees for preaching the resurrection of Christ from the dead. They were kept in prison overnight and then brought before magistrates, elders and scribes and questioned harshly as to whose power and authority they used to heal. The same Peter who was terribly frightened by a slave girl in the courtyard when Jesus was taken prisoner now boldly spoke forth. He said they healed through the power and authority of Jesus Christ of Nazareth, whom the Jews had crucified, yet God raised Him up from the dead! After much private discussion, the temple officials were at a loss as to what to do with Peter and John, so they threatened them and forbid them to speak any more of the name of Jesus and sent them away.

After they were allowed to go, Peter and John returned to their own company and told them everything that had happened. In verse 24 (Acts 4, AMP), having heard all, the believers lifted their voices together with one united mind to God, calling out in prayer that He would grant His servants full freedom to declare His message fearlessly.

Acts 4:31-37 says that *"when they had prayed, the place was shaken where they were assembled together; and they were all filled with the Holy Ghost, and they spake the word of God with boldness. And the multitude of them that believed were of one heart and of one soul:*

neither said any of them that ought of the things which he possessed was his own; but they had all things common. And with great power gave the apostles witness of the resurrection of the Lord Jesus: and great grace was upon them all. Neither was there any among them that lacked: for as many as were possessors of lands or houses sold them, and brought the prices of the things that were sold, And laid them down at the apostles' feet: and distribution was made unto every man according as he had need. And Joses, who by the apostles was surnamed Barnabas, (which is, being interpreted, The son of consolation,) a Levite, and of the country of Cyprus, Having land, sold it, and brought the money, and laid it at the apostles' feet" (KJV).

Can you honestly think of a church today in America where the individual members would give up all of their possessions to be used by all? Probably not, for only the cults of these days are doing that. In fact, if a mainline church did that today, they would probably be branded a religious cult and suffer all kinds of wrong things said about them.

Acts 4:33 (AMP) tells us that the apostles had great strength and ability and power to preach of the resurrection of Jesus Christ, and great grace rested richly upon everyone in this company of believers. Verse 34 tells us that there was not one destitute or needy person among them. Those who had land or houses sold them and brought the proceeds and laid it at the feet of the apostles who caused distribution to be made according to whoever had true need. This is a great example of the power of right agreement, agreement with the leading of the Holy Ghost. Once every person in this group came into one heart, one soul, one united mind, God caused power and ability to flow through the apostles to preach of Christ's resurrection and great grace rested richly upon them.

Ananias and Sapphira

At this time there was a certain man named Ananias and his wife Sapphira who sold a piece of their property and made a wrong agreement to lie about the amount of the sale. Rather than choose to give only what they wanted to give, they hid part of the proceeds of the sale for their own use, and then Ananias took the rest and lay it at the apostles' feet saying it was their all. Peter was anointed of the Holy Ghost, for he knew what they had done. He was quite angry with Ananias for lying about the amount of money the land had been sold for. Ananias was obviously trying to present himself as having given everything he had, as others were doing to help with the common cause of all. In presenting his land sale as such, he implied he was acting under the influence of the Holy Spirit.

He was trying to use the Holy Spirit as part of his wrong agreement. Bad choice! How could Ananias believe that the Holy Spirit would allow himself to be misrepresented in wrong agreement with this liar? How was Ananias so deceived, especially in the presence of the divine power and anointing of so many who were in right agreement? Wrong agreement always produces darkness and evil.

Acts 5:2-5 tell us, *"With his wife's full knowledge he kept back part of the money for himself, but brought the rest and put it at the apostles' feet. Then Peter said, 'Ananias, how is it that Satan has so filled your heart that you have lied to the Holy Spirit and have kept for yourself some of the money you received for the land? Didn't it belong to you before it was sold? And after it was sold, wasn't the money at your disposal? What made you think of doing such a thing? You have not lied to men but to God.' When Ananias heard this, he fell down and died. And great fear seized all who heard what had happened"* (NIV).

We begin to read of Sapphira's part in this in Acts 5:7-11, *"About three hours later his wife came in, not knowing what had happened. Peter asked her, 'Tell me, is this the price you and Ananias got for the land?' 'Yes,' she said, 'that is the price.' Peter said to her, 'How could you agree to test the Spirit of the Lord? Look! The feet of the men who buried your husband are at the door, and they will carry you out also.' At that moment she fell down at his feet and died. Then the young men came in and, finding her dead, carried her out and buried her beside her husband. Great fear seized the whole church and all who heard about these events"* (NIV).

Peter pronounced judgment on Ananias and Sapphira for lying in one accord. Because they were in perfect wrong agreement *(sumphoneo)*, they were both equally guilty of the same crime. You can soulishly agree with others who are wrong in an action and be equally guilty of the error (crime, lie, dishonesty) they have committed.

In those times, wives were never given a chance to speak on such things. They were more or less considered property of their husbands. As such, they would quite likely suffer their husbands' negative fate without even being asked about their part in such a circumstance. But we see Peter here asking Sapphira to tell him if the amount of money given was the complete price of the house. Peter actually seems to be giving Sapphira a chance to come clean and disassociate herself from the wrong agreement she had entered into with her husband. I believe if Sapphira had done so and repented, she might have escaped the judgment of the wrong agreement that had just caused her husband to lose his life.

Wrong agreement between this husband and wife brought about both of their deaths. Wrong agreement never brings forth good results, even if the wrong agreement is entered into in the name of a wife's submission to her husband. Those who have ears to hear, let them hear.

Do You Trust God and His Word?

We must learn to commit ourselves to praying in agreement with the Word, laying aside all personal feelings and opinions about what God does or does not want. I have prayed with people and bound their will to the will of God, that His will would be done. I've seen fear and doubt in their expressions as I said amen. I knew they were thinking, "But what if it isn't His will to—heal me—get me out of debt—save my relationship—get me out of this job, etc.?" This is always a sign of a much deeper problem, the source being this person has never learned that God can be trusted to always do the right thing.

Too many think that God did say a good thing to Jeremiah (29:11), while it doesn't apply to them personally: *"For I know the plans I have for you, declares the LORD, plans to prosper you and not to harm you, plans to give you hope and a future"* (NIV). When we connect this to 2 Timothy 3:16-17, we read, ***"All Scripture is God-breathed and is useful*** *for* *teaching, rebuking, correcting and training in righteousness, so that the man of God may be thoroughly equipped for every good work"* (NIV). If these two verses don't settle doubt and fear about the goodness of God and comfort us, we come back to the bottom line problem of not really trusting God to always act towards us in goodness.

I remember when I first began to read the Bible, I would pull things terribly out of context and claim all sorts of promises, and fear all sorts of judgments. More mature believers were constantly trying to tell me that I couldn't claim this (it was for the Israelites in the Old Testament), and no, that didn't apply to me (the judgment on the Pharoah of Egypt of the Old Testament), and so on. I became so confused for awhile, I almost decided that I couldn't believe in anything in the book of Romans, for it was for the Roman Christians of the New Testament, and the promises in Ephesians were for the Ephesian Christians of the New Testament, etc. Eventually I did stop claiming things I wasn't sure of, but I made up my mind I was going to personally appropriate and believe every single Scripture in the Bible that seemed to strengthen my faith and belief that God loved me—Romans, Ephesians, Corinthians, Timothy, Psalms, Proverbs, Abraham, Isaac, and Jacob! Mine, all mine.

We must all come to a place where we are seeking how to pray in accordance with the will of God. The personal filters of individual unsurrendered souls will always try to tweak the high goal of agreeing with His will alone. As Christians,we exalt ourselves far above our actual position with God when we think or say that we know exactly what His will is in this situation or that problem. We can all look back on so many of the characters in the Bible and see the outcome of God's will with such "anointed" hindsight. We often believe we have an overly "anointed" foresight on what God is doing as well.

Daniel Submitted and Prospered

While in captivity to King Nebuchadnezzar, Daniel was confronted with a royal order to eat of the diet of the king's palace. But he believed this would defile him. So, Daniel <u>requested</u> of the chief of the king's eunuchs that he might be allowed to not defile himself with the palace food (Daniel 1:8 AMP). God extended favor, compassion, and loving kindness to Daniel through the chief of the eunuchs (vs. 9). Amazingly, Daniel was allowed to prove the wisdom of his own dietary choices even though this official feared the reprisal of the king if Daniel and his friends suffered poor health (vs. 10). The rest of the story is that King Nebuchadnezzar was highly impressed with Daniel, and his three friends who ate the same diet as Daniel, when they were compared with other young men brought before him who were eating the palace food.

What had the most impact upon the outcome of this situation? Did Daniel assert his authority and power as one of God's people, commanding respect for himself because of his divine connections? Did Daniel assert his authority and power to stand off the forces of darkness in spiritual warfare? Or, was it God who (in response to Daniel's quiet and respectful obedience and surrender to His ways) divinely caused those around Daniel to show him great favor? It was God, of course. You see, God was in the process of doing something that neither the other Hebrew young men nor Daniel was aware of. God was divinely placing Daniel into a position of influence within the Babylonian kingdom for future use.

Unfortunately, many Christians today would believe that their status as a child of God would give them the right to take a stand against the offending "authority," and they would feel totally rationalized, justified, and sanctified in doing so. How often do we frustrate the same divine plan laid out here for Daniel when God wants to place us into positions of influence with the most unusual of people—positions He has marked for future purposes? When we assert our "rights" as a child of God, we may close all doors to any further Kingdom influence we might have had upon certain people. We may be "branded" in their eyes as religious extremists or just plain nuts. More on that later.

I believe that Daniel had great influence with King Nebuchadnezzar, not because of great personal charisma or soul power, but because of his calm submission to authority while he radiated peaceful wisdom from above. When the king was later troubled in his sleep and filled with dreams, he sent for his magicians, sorcerers, and diviners to tell him what the dreams had been. They could not, saying that no one but the gods could do that—gods who obviously did not dwell among flesh. The one true God was positioning everyone for a supernatural intervention in the natural order of things.

The failure of the sorcerers and diviners so infuriated Nebuchadnezzar (Daniel 2:12), he ordered all of the wise men of Babylon to be killed. The decree went forth to round them all up and bring them before the king. The palace officers brought in Daniel and his companions as well. Upon learning the details of the urgency of the situation, Daniel went before the king and asked for time to interpret the dream for him.

Urgent Prayers of Agreement

When granted such a wish by the king, Daniel went back to his house and told his three Hebrew companions what he had done and *"urged them to plead for mercy from the God of heaven concerning this mystery, so that he and his friends might not be executed with the rest of the wise men of Babylon"* (Daniel 2:18, NIV). Daniel was asking them for **agreement in prayer** that God in His mercy would reveal the meaning of the king's dream to them to save the lives of many. By morning, God had answered this prayer and revealed the dream to Daniel.

Would we call Daniel a religious extremist for believing that he and his friends could **pray in agreement** and have God reveal the secret that could save the lives of all of the wise men of Babylon? Of course we wouldn't, because we know the end of the story. But let's say that tomorrow a young, unknown evangelist used the medium of television to urge the Church to join with him in a 24-hour, non-stop prayer of agreement that God in His mercy give revelation on how to bring all murder and cruelty in the world to a halt. Would the entire Church believe him and (without one single Christian exempting themselves) come together and pray 24 hours straight for God to give this revelation to this young evangelist? Realistically, no. There would be a general consensus that he was just a little over zealous, but God would bring him into maturity some day. And everyone would go right on with religious business as usual.

There is no inherent holiness or blessing in our being branded as a religious extremist, <u>except for one reason only</u>: when this "branding" results from our total abandonment of all of our own personal desires and expectations in complete obedience and surrender to finding and then obeying God's will. We must obey God simply for the pure sake of obedience, regardless of the outcome of our act of obedience. This is the only form of "religious" extremism we should seek to be identified with. W. Glyn Evans, author of *Daily with the King* (Moody Press), says this: "To (simply) do God's will is the disciple's function, and God does not always make His will clear before hand. . . . I must learn what Jesus learned: to be *'obedient unto death'* (Phil. 2:8, KJV). <u>All true obedience is unto death.</u>"

True obedience is a reversal of the world's standard. "I will obey *if* . . . ," is what the world says. Christ's example was, "I will obey regardless." <u>True obedience</u> will always see "the goal" as accomplishing God's will. No expectations of rewards—just obedience to God's will. Beyond that goal, everything else is God's business.

Would You Have Known?

So many of our determinations about what God wants or doesn't want us to do, with regard to the sin we see around us, has to do with conclusions reached by our finite minds (human reasoning, however knowledgeable, yet devoid of divine influence). For instance:

·   Do you think that you would have known God's will regarding the initial captivity of Daniel? Or would you have prayed against the devil and

> commanded the "spirit of Nebuchadnezzar" to free Daniel from the clutches of darkness?

- Do you think you would have known God's will regarding Nebuchadnezzar putting Shadrach, Meshach, and Abednego into the fiery furnace?

- Do you think you would have known God's will regarding the crucifixion of Christ?

Agreement Prayer

Father, we come to you now with great expectation and hope in our souls and our spirits. We come to you by choice and in the fullest agreement we know how to enact as the members of your sometimes fractious body. Jesus, as our Head, we bind our minds to your mind, asking for your grace and anointing to complete our commitment to this commission. God, we stand on and believe your promise in 2 Chronicles 7:14 (KJV) that if we, your people, will humble ourselves, and pray, and seek your face, and turn from our wicked ways; then will you hear from heaven, and will forgive our sin, and will heal our land.

As Christians, we are the people who are called by your name, Jesus. We now choose to humble ourselves individually, and in corporate agreement, and to pray and seek your face. You have said we are to turn from our wicked ways. We will not try to rationalize or justify our ways, defending ourselves as moral and righteous people. We will admit we have failed terribly in a consistent walking in love toward this world and towards our Christian brothers and sisters.

Your Word says that we shall be known by our love for one another. Yet, so often we bite at one another through strife over personal rights and expectations. Forgive me and forgive us, Jesus. We have built fortified strongholds of doctrinal division, seeing ourselves as having the most truth. We have empowered the forces of darkness by coming into wrong agreements with and even about others, Jesus.

Father, we are praying that your will would be done in the following areas. In us, in the body of Christ, in others, in the unsaved, in the government, in families, in every area of life here on earth. We agree that your will and your will alone shall be the focus of our prayers. Lord, we bind ourselves to your will and to the truth of your Word. We loose all of our own human conclusions and expectations out of our souls as we pray in agreement.

We bind the government leaders of our country and of the world to your will and to the truth of your Word. We loose the hold of all of their human conclusions and expectations from their souls. We loose the power and effects of the wrong agreements they have voluntarily made or felt coerced to make. We loose wrong counsel of others from them. We ask that your will be done in their lives, in their families, in their decisions, in their motives, and in their agendas. We ask that your will be done on earth as you have so established it in heaven.

Jesus, we bind the spiritual leaders of our own cities, our own states, of our country, of Israel, and of the world, to your will and to the truth of your Word. We loose the hold of all soulish conclusions and personal expectations from their souls. We loose the

211

power and effects of the wrong agreements they have voluntarily made or felt coerced to make. We loose wrong counsel of others from them. We ask that your will be done in their lives, in their families, in their decisions, in their motives, and in their agendas. We ask that your will be done on earth as you have so established it in heaven

Jesus, every member of every family of every person who will pray this prayer, we bind them to your will and to the truth of your Word. We loose the hold of all soulish conclusions and personal expectations from each soul represented by ties to those who will pray this prayer. Nothing good or permanent will ever come from human conclusions that exclude divine grace. Nothing good or permanent will ever come from human expectations of other humans, good only comes from you.

We loose the power and effects of the wrong agreements from each one of these souls represented by ties to those who will pray this prayer. Lord, we shatter and crush all of the fallout and effects from these wrong agreements that they have voluntarily made or felt coerced to make. We loose wrong counsel of others from them. We ask that your will be done in their lives, in their families, in their decisions, in their motives, and in their agendas.

We ask that you will arrange circumstances and situations around them to cause them to see your face. We ask that you will minister healing and hope to them, and help them to open up to you to receive grace and mercy in the hidden areas of their souls—the areas of their worst fears, their worst pain, their deepest needs. We ask that your will be done on earth in their lives as you have so established it in heaven.

Lord, we bind every Christian in the body of Christ to your will regarding your provision and your promises. We bind their wills to your will, we bind their minds to the mind of Christ, we bind them to the truth of the Word. Help them to know that money means nothing to you. Rather, you are concerned about what money means to us and to them. Help every one of your children to understand that money won't buy healing, won't buy grace, won't buy love, won't buy divine favor, won't buy Kingdom positioning. Help them to seek first the Kingdom of God, loosing all fear and doubt about money, and let you take care of that. We loose all wrong beliefs, wrong teachings, wrong agreements, wrong attitudes about money from every Christian in the body of Christ. We loose all wrong ideas we may have about why we deserve certain answers and about why we are not seeming to receive what we have interpreted as promises we have a right to expect you to fulfill whether we change or not.

We bind every single person in this country to your will and we loose the wrong thinking and beliefs from their souls that have caused them to come into wrong agreements. Every single person, every race and culture, all ages, men and women, rich and poor, from streetwise to university educated, <u>every single person in this country</u> needs to think in one accord with you, Jesus. Those who have themselves felt oppressed, have ancestors who have been oppressed, have felt the sting of prejudice or ignorance, have had possessions unjustly stripped from them, have experienced strong emotional reactions to others who are "different" from them, Lord, we bind their minds to the mind of Christ. We loose the effects and influences of the negative agreements they have entered into with each other regarding their fear, their losses, their grief, their pain,

213

their anger, and their hatred towards those who were responsible or who are just seemingly "like" those who were responsible.

Father, show us how to always pray in agreement for the one result that is always right: <u>Your will be done on earth as you have so set it in heaven</u>. You have chosen us to be the instruments of what you want to manifest on earth. What an awesome responsibility you have entrusted us with and how we have fallen short of fulfilling it up until now. We will change! Amen.

9

Warfare in the Heavenlies

Mini Refresher Course on Spirits

The church world is too willing today to blame things on the devil and his spirits. I think Satan is probably quite amused by this focus on him. In Chapter Three of *Breaking the Power,* I have addressed several of the uses of the word spirit in the Old Testament that appear to be evil spirits, yet are actually bad attitudes out of the human soul when studied in the original Hebrew wording. I did not include the so-called "spirit of fear" from the New Testament in that chapter, but will briefly address this phrase here because so many people have been taught to believe that there is a demon or spirit of fear. This wrong teaching encourages fearful people to believe that their fears are the works of a demon which can be cast out of them. This erroneous belief usually comes from 2 Timothy 1:7 which tells us that *"God hath not given us the spirit of fear; but of power, and of love, and of a sound mind"* (KJV). I believe a better version of this verse is found in the NIV translation, *"For God did not give us a spirit of timidity, but a spirit of power, of love and of self-discipline."* Not many deliverance ministries would be nearly as inclined to believe that a spirit of timidity was a demonic spirit.

The Greek word translated as *spirit* in 2 Timothy 1:7 is *pneuma* (Strong's/Thayers #4151:5). Thayer's Greek/English Lexicon describes *pneuma* as used in 2 Timothy 1:7 as meaning "to be filled with the same spirit as Christ, and by the bond of that spirit to be intimately united to Christ." In other words, our human spirits cannot fear because of their intimate bond to the Spirit of Christ. Regenerated spirits have no room for fear, they are too full of Christ's overcoming power.

Fear is a negative emotional reaction out of the soul, generally a powerful reaction to pressure upon an unresolved traumatic issue long rooted in that soul. Fear is not a spirit, it is a symptom of an internal source in the soul that needs healing. As long as the wrong belief, wrong understanding, or unresolved issue exists, the enemy knows exactly how to pressure it today with copycat circumstances of the circumstance (from the past) that birthed it in the first place. The internal source or root cause that has torn open a fearful individual's sense of security and courage must be <u>voluntarily exposed to God</u> before He will reach into it and heal. He will not fight your soul's defense systems to heal you. The binding and loosing prayer principles are very effective in dismantling these defense systems to open up the scariest hiding place.

Strong's definition of the original Greek word *deilos* (#1169, di-los'), translated as fear, means being timid and faithless (having no trust and confidence in the goodness of God's intentions towards you). The same word is translated as fearful in Revelation 21:8, being further translated in the Amplified Version of the Bible as lacking in courage.

In Joshua 1:9, God said to Joshua, *"Have not I commanded thee? Be strong and of a good courage; be not afraid, neither be thou dismayed: for the LORD thy God is with thee whithersoever thou goest"* (KJV). Psalms 27:14 tells us to *"Wait on the LORD: be of good courage, and he shall strengthen thine heart: wait, I say, on the LORD"* (KJV). The Hebrew word for courage means to be to be alert, steadfastly minded, strong and established, and to prevail (amongst other meanings). Courage in the Greek of the New Testament means confidence. These are attributes all growing out of faith, having trust and confidence in the goodness of God. Courage is not achieved in a fearful soul by a casting out of any evil spirit.

Having already covered this subject in some depth in *Breaking the Power* (Chapter Three), I now prefer to go on to further understanding of how humans continue to empower the forces of darkness to badger them, to harrass the body of Christ, and to bring pain and destruction to the rest of the world.

Deliverance and Deliverance Ministries

I have found myself in unusual circumstances from time to time when God has exercised His sense of humor and caused deliverance ministries to invite me to teach their flock. Usually these ministries really don't know what I'm about, nor do I know what they are about, which is God's little joke. We sometimes end up having three or four rather awkward days together, but we all survive the experience and are probably more enlightened for it. I believe most deliverance ministers are sincerely wanting to be helpful, but I believe they are usually sincerely wrong in how they are going about it. I do not believe pastors should ever allow or practice deliverance on people in their church services. There is no evidence anywhere in the Bible that Jesus Christ or any one of the apostles or disciples ever conducted a deliverance service in a New Testament Church setting.

Some churches and ministries regularly practice deliverance on members and staff. I do not find any basis for this anywhere in the New Testament Church. Every one of the deliverances performed on individuals in the New Testament (by Christ, an apostle, or a disciple) was always on an unbeliever. Never a believer. Christ and the apostles and the disciples were generally too busy preaching the Good News of the Gospel to set up special times to deal with evil spirits. However, woe be unto the evil spirit who ended up crossing their paths while they were about the Father's business in other ways. The spirits were not argued with or even dialogued with, they were simply dispatched. Get out, leave, be gone, hit the road, summed up most of the deliverance practices of the New Testament.

Some people have come to me relating examples of having seen demons cast out of Christians. I tell them I don't doubt that. The easiest and fastest way I know to relate why I say that, since I do not believe that Christians can have demons, is the result of two occasions where I have seen wrong agreements take place to give some form of entrance or overpowering of a Christian by a demon. In the first instance, while speaking at a conference for an independent ministry, I was called along with the other speakers to come forth for prayer. I was not comfortable with the direction I sensed the prayer line was probably heading towards, but I went forward. I heard the minister (who had called us to come) begin to pray over the speakers to my right, commanding demonic spirits to leave them alone and depart from them. As I was wondering how to get out of the line before he got to me, I suddenly "saw" within my mind a horrible demonic face. I was incredibly startled, briefly wondering if there might actually be a demonic spirit in me.

As I usually do when I'm caught off guard by anything, I immediately bound my will to the will of God and bound my mind to the mind of Christ. Then I loosed all wrong patterns of thinking and the effects and influences of wrong agreements from myself and the face disappeared just as quickly as it had appeared. As the well-meaning minister approached me, I kept binding my mind to the mind of Christ as he laid his hands on my head. He paused thoughtfully and then said, "Bless you, sister," and moved past me.

What do I think occurred? I believe that the man was actually discerning demonic spirits present, spirits that probably followed him to this meeting knowing he would give them opportunity to see some action. As the minister prayed over each other person in the line, he asked that person to agree with him that certain spirits on (in, around, over, behind, betwixt, whatever) him or her would have to leave. As soon as the people being prayed for came into those wrong agreements with him, spirits were on them (under them, around them, behind them, whatever), and the man truly did then command spirits to leave them. Do I think he was deliberately trying to fake something or bring anyone into danger?

No, I do not. I think he was quite sincere. But I think he was bringing each person in that line into dangerous agreement that allowed darkness to settle directly upon them, however briefly. When he came to me, he could not sense any agreement within me and he moved on. That is one reason I believe he was very sincere in what he was doing—when there was no agreement, he did not try to force it.

Demons Go to Church

On another occasion, I unexpectedly had a Sunday night free on the road. Having heard about a large church in the area, I attended the evening service. I had just finished several days of intense teaching, and I planned to sneak into the back of this church and let someone feed me. As I entered the foyer, I was not happy to see a big banner trumpeting their bi-monthly, Sunday night deliverance service. Since someone had dropped me off at the church and I did not want to call a cab, I sighed and went on in. Upon entering the sanctuary I was instantly aware that the place was filled with demonic spirits. They were "floating" all over the place! Doesn't it seem that demonic spirits would want to be as far away from a deliverance service as possible?

To add to my discomfort, I was recognized by the pastor and he called me to come forward and sit on the front row. My sneak-in-the-back plans went poof as I went down front, smiling painfully. Following a good song service, the minister began to call people forward to effect (work, minister, practice, invoke, whatever) deliverance upon them. I watched him press people for agreement that there was a demonic spirit in them (on, under, over, around, whatever) and they were ready to get rid of it. As each person agreed with him, I saw spirits appear to "enter" the person. Then the minister legitimately cast spirits out of them (off of them, away from them, whatever). These Christians manifested all the symptoms of the "traditional" demonic possession deliverance: arched backs, clawed hands, gutteral voices, feet appearing to levitate off the floor, and vomiting into waste baskets. Satan has always initiated his works of darkness through the souls of men and women. Whenever he can tempt your soul into wrong agreement with his deceptions, your body will manifest related responses.

This is a very dangerous situation for the person who comes into such a wrong agreement. Wrong agreement always allows forces of darkness to encroach upon territory they have no business encroaching upon. I cannot say the demonic spirits have no right to do this, for the wrong agreement gives them the right. I can only say that I hope those who are practicing this deception truly do know how to cast all of the spirits off or out of those they have caused to open up to darkness through their wrong agreements.

I do not believe a Christian can be possessed by the devil. Possession means total control and ownership. You cannot partly "belong" to Christ and partly "belong" to the devil. However, if a person has enough unresolved issues, enough unhealed hurts, enough unmet needs, and multiple open doors for spirits to hammer on them, then terrified, deeply wounded, and/ or anger-filled Christians can act "possessed." The unsurrendered soul will sometimes cooperate with these manifestations if it feels such acting out will help derail an impending discovery of its culpability in opening up the whole mess in the first place.

I do believe in deliverance from demonic spirits, but I think this is not what we are seeing practiced in our churches today. We are seeing demonic side shows.

Breaking Strongholds Over Our Cities

It is not always easy to prepare ourselves to receive God's revelation understanding as purely as He wants to give it. We are still earthen vessels, and often prone to wanting to interpret God's words and issues our own way (which is sin). First John 3:3 (AMP) tells us sin is " . . . *being unrestrained and unregulated by His commands and His will."*

The intent of my teaching on praying with binding and loosing principles has always been to explain how the keys of the Kingdom can be used to stabilize the Christian's will and focus the Christian's mind while loosing all hindrances to praying the only perfect prayer: *"Thy will be done, O Lord."* Try as we might to achieve that perfect prayer, we all struggle at times to let God *"color outside the lines"* of our souls' understanding. The Lord speaks most freely to those who can honestly admit that the more they learn about Him and His ways, the less they know of His eternal-minded, yet very present-tense, plans and purposes for their lives and the rest of the world.

With the world in the state it is, why are we not yet experiencing spiritual revival that turns cities, government leaders, schools, and families upside down (or right side up) across our land? Many are praying around the world, asking God for an outpouring of His presence, and we are seeing some visitations of His Spirit in certain areas. This is evidenced by huge numbers of Christians flocking to these areas hoping to see what spiritual revival looks like. I do not believe that the different "pre-revival" manifestations of His presence we've seen so far have happened in a random manner, with God just showing up here and there to bless. Someone has been breaking wrong agreements over those areas and pushing back territorial darkness. (By "pre-revival," I mean that we have not yet come close to the outpouring of God's end-time revival manifestations that will come.)

God's end times spiritual revival will not be to bring warm fuzzy blessings to Christians, it will be a white-hot shaft of fire and light in the midst of great shaking. Following the words of Paul regarding Christ's covenant of grace for believers (Hebrews 12:18-24), Peterson's *The Message* interprets Paul's instructions (Hebrews 12:25-29) regarding God's end times warnings in this way: *"Don't turn a deaf ear to these gracious words. If those who ignored earthly warnings didn't get away with it, what will happen to us if we turn our backs on heavenly warnings? His voice that time shook the earth to its foundations; this time—He's told us quite plainly—He'll also rock the heavens: 'One last shaking, from top to bottom, stem to stern.' The phrase 'one last shaking' means a thorough house cleaning, getting rid of all the historical and religious junk so that the unshakable essentials stand clear and uncluttered. Do you see what we've got? An unshakable kingdom! And do you see how thankful we must be? Not only thankful, but brimming with worship, deeply reverent before God. For God is not an indifferent bystander. He's actively cleaning house, torching all that needs to burn, and He won't quit until it's all cleansed. God himself is Fire!"*

Pray First Where You Are

In the early part of 1987, I attended a Mario Murillo meeting on the extreme backside of a mountain in Northern California. I had convinced several others to drive approximately 80 miles into the mountains with me for this service. I urged them to go, telling them we would all get a real blessing. We storm-trooped into the meeting right on time, sort of basking in our efforts and investment of our time, shared expenses, and twisting mountain driving to be in attendance.

Brother Mario promptly slam-dunked all of us shortly after we had arrived, saying: "Christians in America are running all around the land wherever they think the latter rain is falling and grass is springing up to bless them. You need to squat down in the dry dust of your own cities and pray for the rain to fall until the grass springs up where you are!" Ouch, we all said. I had experienced his rather brusk way of cutting to the chase before and was not offended, but my fellow attendees were not so inclined to be that charitable towards him.

I did feel a little stung myself, yet I was strangely intrigued by the prospects of going back home and trying to do just what he'd said. I find it hard to believe now that this wake-up call appeared to be such a new revelation. I promptly started an intercessors' group that has met each week in my home or offices since 1987 (with extremely rare exceptions). Some of the intercessors have changed, but the current "core group" has stayed the same since *Shattering Your Strongholds* was being birthed during 1991 and 1992.

Within this group, we are still trying to grow and reach beyond our established focus of prayer. We know that it is way past time to begin to raise the stakes personally and locally, and to kick up the intensity level of our prayer focus both nationally and globally. Jesus Christ spoke to chosen apostles (Acts 1:2) after His resurrection, saying, *"Ye shall receive power, after that the Holy Ghost is come upon you: and ye shall be witnesses unto me both in Jerusalem, and in all Judaea, and in Samaria, and unto the uttermost part of the earth"* (Acts 1:8, KJV). All of us are called to obey this command to pray, to witness, to stay, to go, to do whatever His will is for us.

In order to fulfill 2 Chronicles 7:14, *"If my people, which are called by my name, shall humble themselves, and pray, and seek my face, and turn from their wicked ways; then will I hear from heaven, and will forgive their sin, and will heal their land"* (KJV), a concerted effort of prayer agreement needs to be sought. Too often Christians do not place themselves into the context of this Scripture, refusing to recognize their own "wicked" ways. In the original Hebrew, the word wicked used in this verse means (in part) bad, disagreeable, unpleasant, pain causing, displeasing, unkind <u>thoughts, deeds, and actions</u>. Could anyone in the body of Christ today honestly not see at least a few of their "ways" here? We all want to believe that wickedness is pornography, murder, adultery, stealing, etc. When we create our own rules for judging wickedness, we can judge ourselves as not included in the *"turn from their wicked ways"* portion of this verse's command from God.

Our country desperately needs prayers of agreement that *God's will be done in earth as it is in heaven* (Matthew 6:10, Luke 11:2). Our ministry prayer group began with a local prayer invasion, twenty-one days of prayer focused on binding the people of our area of Northern California to the will and purposes of God and loosing the influences and effects of wrong agreements from them. We zeroed in on dismantling and demolishing the dominion hold that territorial spirits had set up and <u>protected</u> with territorial strongholds in an area of approximately 30 by 70 miles.

This ministry has concentrated on three areas of effort over the past year, both locally and nationally: 1) preaching and teaching about Jesus' instructions on keys of the Kingdom praying, 2) preaching and teaching about the Christians' responsibilities to produce the promises of God by prayer, and 3) practicing and producing the spiritual birthing of natural manifestations of God's will through right prayer. Preaching, teaching, practicing, and producing God's will on earth through praying steadily in scriptural agreement in one accord to dethrone the princes of the air over our city has begun shaking the foundations of their power structures. We have seen breakthroughs in our ministry, but we are praying for still more to join us with right agreement for the entire area.

Focusing

Ephesians 3:10 (NIV) tells us, *"His intent was that now, through the church, the manifold wisdom of God should be made known to the rulers and authorities in the heavenly realms."* What a great verse. God's intent was and still is that the Church, the body of Christ, should rise up and through their words and actions reveal God's manifold wisdom to the rulers and authorities in the air!

Ephesians 6:12 (KJV) tells us, *"We wrestle not*

against flesh and blood, but against principalities, against powers, against the rulers of the darkness of this world, against spiritual wickedness in high places. " We have had our focus in the wrong places. The "high places" referred to here are not human power structures, rather Strong's Greek dictionary reveals these power structures are placed high above the sky in celestial places. Thayer tells us that the term "principalities" was transferred by the Apostle Paul in his writings meaning angels or demons holding dominions that have been entrusted to them in the order of things. The particular dominions of Ephesians 6:12 are definitely demonic.

Whose <u>order of things</u> established this turning over of power to such forces? Colossians 1:16-17 (KJV) tells us, *"By <u>him</u>* (Christ) *were all things created, that are in heaven, and that are in earth, visible and invisible, whether they be thrones, or dominions, or principalities, or powers: all things were created by him, and for him. And he is before all things, and by him all things consist. "* My, my, my. Obviously some rather nasty creatures have been allowed into places of power and will remain there until God's people present God's manifold wisdom to them. I believe the following paragraphs will reveal what allows these power set ups over an area, what empowers them while they are in place, and how to strip them of their right to stay.

Victory: Conquering + Occupying

Most Christians have experienced some victory in their battles with demonic forces, even if the "victory" was conceded by Satan just to keep them interested in fighting fights they never had to fight in the first place.

All too often the victories genuinely won (as well as those conceded) soon evaporate, and the opportunities to occupy and hold the territories disappear. Christians must follow up spiritual triumphs by being *"more than conquerors* (Romans 8:37)." We must conquer and then occupy that which we have won. To drive an enemy from an area is rarely a permanent solution. The vacancy created must be occupied by filling it with what is good. You must occupy the territorial grounds of any victory to keep it from being recaptured.

Ephesians 4:27 (AMP) tells us what happens if we disobey the command of God in verse 26, which says we must not let the sun go down on our anger. This is a command that I believe every Christian in the body of Christ has broken, and often continues to break day after day. When we are in disobedience to this command of the Father, verse 27 (AMP) says we have just given the devil room, opportunity, and a foothold in our lives. Here are the doors of access through which evil spirits attack born again, blood washed Christians in spite of their authority in Christ, in spite of their blood covering from Christ, in spite of their righteous stands in Christ.

Authority, protection, and right standing in any area of life, natural or spiritual, can be severely hindered, even rendered useless, by the presence of open doors that an enemy can come and go through as he will. Leaders in the armed forces of the U.S. will tell you that their highest levels of authority, protection, and rights are useless if there are open doors in their supply sources, communication lines, planning rooms, and secret battle plans. There isn't a smart enemy alive who won't use those open doors to attack, slash, and burn— and the Christian's enemy is very smart. Don't ever be foolish enough to call him stupid, or to sing foolish songs about him. Jude 1:8-9 states, *"In the very same way, these dreamers pollute their own bodies, reject authority and slander celestial beings. But even the archangel Michael, when he was disputing with the devil about the body of Moses, did not dare to bring a slanderous accusation against him, but said, 'The Lord rebuke you!'"* (NIV).

Right Alignment For End Time Assignment

Territorial spirits, principalities, and powers in high places find their access into or over geographical areas through the power released to them from multiplied negative agreements of the souls of those in the area. It is a natural human desire to seek validation agreement with our negative emotions. This is especially true when the emotions are powerful and intense, such as grief, loss, anger, fear, bitterness, betrayal, unforgiveness, hatred, desire for revenge, etc.

In Daniel 1, we read of one of the largest deportations ever of God's people. This occurred when the king of Babylon besieged Jerusalem. The Lord did not just allow this to happen, He caused it to happen. This is a "hard thing" for many Christians to accept, that God will cause traumatic things to happen in the lives of His people because they remain in disobedience to His repeated commands. Hear what Jeremiah 27:5-7 (AMP) tells us God said about His people: *"I have made the earth, the men and the beasts that are upon the face of the earth, by My great power and by My outstretched arm, and I give it to whom it seems right and suitable to Me. And now I have given all these lands into the hand of Nebuchadnezzar the king of Babylon, My servant and instrument, and the beasts of the field also I have given him to serve him. And all nations shall serve him and his son and his grandson, until the God-appointed time of punishment of his own land comes. . . . So do not listen to your false prophets . . . who say to you, You shall not serve the king of Babylon. For they prophesy a lie to you, which will cause you to be removed far from your land, and I will drive you out, and you will perish."*

The king of Judah was "given" into the hands of Nebuchadnezzar, along with gold articles of the house of God. Nebuchadnezzar then carried away the wealthiest and most skilled Israelites into exile—all of the officers, fighting men, craftsmen, artisans, leaving only the poorest people of the land behind. Loss of country and home can occur (even to God's special people) when God chooses to allow it for His higher purposes. Never forget, His thoughts are not our thoughts, nor are our ways His ways. For as the heavens are higher than the earth, so are His ways higher than ours, and His thoughts higher than ours. (See Isaiah 55:9-10.)

This is God's "doing" and who can question Him for it? To know why God does what He does is not for us to inquire of or require answers for. Rather, we need to understand that it is our responsibility to recognize what He expects us to do. To reverse the consequences of captivity and loss is often dependent upon the peoples' "doing" after a loss. In Daniel 9:5-11 (AMP), Daniel prayed and confessed the corporate wrong agreement of his people while in captivity: *"We have sinned and dealt perversely and done wickedly and have rebelled, turning aside from your commandments and ordinances. . . . O Lord, righteousness belongs to you, but to us confusion and shame of face . . . through all the countries to which you have driven them because of the treacherous trespass which they have committed against you . . . . We have not obeyed the voice of our Lord our God by walking in his laws, which he set before us by his servants the prophets . . . . Therefore the curse has been poured out on us, and the oath that is written in the law of Moses the servant of God, because we have sinned against Him. "*

Then Daniel said (9:21-22, AMP): *"While I was speaking and praying, confessing my sin and the sin of my people Israel, and presenting my supplication before the Lord my God . . . Gabriel . . . being caused to fly swiftly, came near to me . . . and said, O Daniel, I am now come forth to give you skill and wisdom and understanding. "*

In Daniel 10:12-13 (AMP), the angel of the Lord says to Daniel: *"Fear not, Daniel, for from the first day that you set your mind and heart to understand and to humble yourself (chasten yourself) before your God, your words were heard, and I have come in consequence of your words. But the prince of the kingdom of Persia withstood me for twenty-one days. But Michael, one of the chief of the celestial princes, came to help me . . . . "*

God's own people were taken into captivity, losing their land, homes, and possessions. The Book of Daniel, 2 Kings, 2 Chronicles, and the Book of Jeremiah all record the warnings of God's messengers that could have prevented this tragic circumstance. God chastised His people after sending message upon message to them of His plans towards them, His pending acts in their lives, and His eternal promises to them. God will always warn His people of any large scale act He is about to

231

take, but His people don't always recognize the truth of His warnings.

In 2 Chronicles 36 and Jeremiah 37, we read that the Israelites became more and more unfaithful to their God, taking up many of the ungodly practices of the Babylonians. God continued to send messages as to how the Israelites could be free of their miserable lot, but they mocked His messengers, despised His words, and scoffed at His prophets while embracing the lies of their false prophets. God's prophet, Jeremiah, was very upset during this time at the number of <u>false prophets telling the captives that all was well, and Babylon would be broken instead of Judah</u>. This is a frightening thought with so many today prophesying wealth and power and unlimited favor for the entire body of Christ. Such wealth and power and favor will not be poured out upon the Church in totality unless there is a massive turning away from so many of our wicked ways.

Another Choice

After speaking vehemently to the Israelites of the false prophets, Jeremiah finally ceased trying to get the true Word of the Lord through to their darkened understanding. He wrote to the Israelites in exile and basically told them to just settle in for the duration of their captivity. In other words, they had made their choice and now they would have to walk out <u>to the bitter end</u> the natural consequences of their earthly circumstances. We always have a choice of our free wills. But if we choose not to hear God's true Word, our free wills may set our feet to walk out hard consequences to a bitter end.

Daniel seemed to understand there was another

choice. He chastened himself and set his heart and mind to understand and pray, and a heavenly battle broke out to dethrone the ungodly "prince of Persia" controlling the principalities over the land. This prince was a territorial spirit who had been given dominion over Babylon because of the multiplied negative emotions of the captives therein. This spirit smothered and blinded the Israelites' reasoning to the point of ignoring God and rejecting His advances of grace. They perpetuated their own bondage, giving authority to the territorial spirit to hold dominion over them because of their continued corporate wrong agreements.

What Does This Have to Do With Us Today?

In America, we have many displaced or "deported" groups, races, and tribes who have been torn from their home lands or had their land torn from them by stronger and more aggressive groups or nations. Why God has allowed this to happen is not known to us, only to Him. God sees a much bigger picture than we do, and our answers do not lie in the why of such things. But such corporate acts of man's inhumanity to man have created and continue creating massive wrong agreements in the minds, wills, and emotions of those who have been oppressed, plundered, enslaved, and wronged. Just as in the days of the Israelites' captivity in Babylon. In the harsh circumstances which have befallen so many tribes, races, nationalities, even philosophical groups, hundreds of thousands of people have come into corporate wrong agreement with one another in their pain, anger, hate, loss, and grief.

God's Word does not permit a sliding scale of choices (based on how wrong something has been) as to whether or not we have a right to be angry and bitter at injustices to ourselves or others. He simply says that none of us are to let the sun go down on our anger. Period. That is such a simple command, yet so very, very difficult for so many of us (if not all of us!).

There are various areas in our nation that have longed for revival, prayed for revival, repented, asked forgiveness from others, sought reconciliation with one another, having great desire for an outpouring of the presence of God in their midst. Yet, having done all they know to do, many are still looking upward with longing while dry and thirsty spiritual land surrounds them. In many areas revival has not come because of the darkness of the territorial spirits feeding off the corporate wrong agreements born out of the fear and pain of people in the area. Perhaps you are one of those who are a part of a corporate group that is plagued with, even consumed by, anger, grief, pain, or fear. Perhaps you are one who simply wants all people to be free. Regardless of who we are, each one of us can be "doing" something in alignment with God's will that will help turn harsh, cruel consequences around wherever we are.

God has said in Isaiah 49:24-25 that captives can be taken back from the terrible one. To do so requires the unseating of the throne of the terrible one holding dominion over the land of the captives. We, the believers, are the ones who have the keys of the Kingdom, given to us by Jesus Christ (Matthew 16:19) with all of His authority behind them to dethrone the powers of darkness residing over our land. This will create an outpouring of grace for corporate right agreement in repentance and prayer, culminating in the healing of our land!

Doing What's Right in God's Eyes

As I travel across America, I have been in direct confrontation with territorial spirits on different occasions. The details of these confrontations are not important here, for the answers do not lie in focusing directly upon warfare with these demonic strongholds, as much as they do with shattering and breaking up the effects and influences of the corporate wrong agreements that are empowering the demonic princes to sit on their thrones. There are powerful demonic strongholds over Sacramento, CA where I live. I am never quite as aware of them as I am when I return from speaking engagements and step off the airplane in the Sacramento airport. From that moment on, through the next 12 to 24 hours, I battle discouragement, depression, and darkness.

The territorial spirits over my city have been feeding off of the corporate wrong agreements of many different groups for a long time. As always, these spirits breathe down darkness, distrust, fear, confusion, and misunderstanding upon the people of the area. More wrong agreements are entered into corporately by groups, and more darkness, distrust, fear, confusion and misunderstanding is breathed down. More wrong agreements follow, and it becomes an almost self-perpetuating cycle.

Many cultural groups, racial groups, tribal groups, and others were betrayed and taken advantage of by those who first came to the Sacramento area. I have studied some of these groups, yet God has not encouraged me to continue to do this. I did not understand why until I ran into other demonic strongholds in other states, and I began to see that these strongholds were symptoms of something else that needed to be confronted. God has told me to preach about what must be dismantled and broken to unseat these spirits. He almost seems to be communicating what I remember saying to my squabbling children when they were were engaged in battling with each other. I can remember telling them, "I don't care who started it, I'm finishing it. I want this ended right now!" God is saying that it doesn't matter who started it, He wants it ended.

He does not look down upon us and see any as having a favorite son or daughter status. He does not see us according to nationality, gender, wealth, education, race, or any other classification that man has come up with. He looks down and sees wounded, hurting, defensive, angry people jockying for power and protection of their self-perceived rights. One group's rights are usually protected at the expense of some other group's rights.

I have preached this message in one church that stands on the very ground of a former African slave holding pen in Alabama and felt the hatred of the territorial forces. It is not hard to imagine the corporate wrong agreements made here out of great fear, pain, grief, loss, anger, and hopelessness. I preached this message in a hotel in Texas where something terrible had to have happened to cause great fear, pain, grief, loss, and anger among the Hispanics, for I actually saw that territorial spirit manifest itself across the sky. Contemplate the corporate wrong agreements made here out of great fear, pain, grief, loss, anger, and hopelessness. I have preached this message in Canada, Washington, and upper Oregon and felt the incredible force of territorial forces over the Pacific Northwest from many different sources. Contemplate the corporate wrong agreements made here out of the great fear, pain, grief, loss, anger, and hopelessess. I have preached this message in Montana and seen powerful breakthrough in the territorial darkness.

In different areas there have been demonic principalities empowered by wrong agreements spoken into place by politcal groups, philosophical groups, economic groups, gender specific groups, wrong lifestyle groups, and many other people groups. Yet, all of the teaching, preaching, and breakthrough this message has brought has come without ever binding or rebuking any evil spirits. It has been accomplished through corporate prayer by all in attendance at meetings, prayers prayed out loud in one accord to loose, shatter, dissolve, and destroy the effects and influences of the wrong agreements of all of the people of the area, as well as former agreements passed on from generation to generation.

If Daniel's prayers that unseated the prince of Persia are a valid pattern for future generations to use to unseat demonic princes over their cities, then let us follow their powerful pattern! Daniel's 21 <u>days</u> of power prayers contained no declaration of authority, no commanding, no rebuking, nor casting down of satanic powers—all actions the unsurrendered soul loves to invoke. His power praying contained only humble confession, repentance, and pleas for mercy regarding the sinfulness of those who had spoken the corporate wrong agreements which drew the prince of Persia into power over Babylon. If church bodies and intercessors' groups across our nation would consider just 21 <u>hours</u> of continuous corporate praying in right agreement after Daniel's fashion, what might happen? I know what I would do. I would pray for God to send me to join at least one group's 21-hour session in every state of our nation.

Corporate Wrong Agreements Perpetuate Fear and Pain

Many peoples' groups have came into intensely wrong (in God's eyes) agreements in their souls. Hurt and hate has been carefully passed from generation to generation, creating new wrong agreements. Massive corporate wrong agreements open the doors to demon-held dominions over geographical areas that <u>continue to perpetuate the distrust, fear, pain, and hatred between people</u>. Although many different cultures and races were oppressed in the early days of Sacramento's history on through into this century (Indians, Blacks, Hispanics, Chinese, etc.), consider this example: There was a Japanese-American "relocation" camp in Sacramento in 1942. This camp imprisoned thousands of Japanese-Americans pulled from their homes and businesses and held before going on to the permanent camps. These Japanese-Americans were made homeless. Sacramento today has a very large homeless population. Sacramento has an ever-increasing record of child abuse, spousal abuse, murder, etc. Sacramento has an ever-growing homosexual and lesbian population. Sacramento has ever-increasing gang activity. Many are at a loss as to how to deal with these problems.

With so much pain, sin, and hopelessness, why has there never been a major spiritual revival in this city? Many of God's people <u>have</u> tried. Many Christians in the hundreds of churches in Sacramento have prayed.

Many have humbled themselves, prayed, sought God's face, and turned from all they recognized as unrighteous. And still the rain of spiritual revival has not fallen upon our city.

I believe that territorial spirits have clouded not only the minds of those who do not know God, but these spirits' intense influences over Sacramento have infiltrated and clouded the minds, wills, and emotions of God's people as well. Wrong agreement has prevailed while many, many attempts to reach total unity and right agreement have failed. This has prevented any <u>sustained occupying</u> of the partial victories that have been won. All too often Christians pray until relief seems to come and then they turn to pray for something else. No occupying of the land is accomplished!

Agreement With Pain Does Not Wipe Pain Away

Finding the answer to the divisions within our society began when many in the body of Christ, and many from outside of it as well, began to turn from their personal mindsets and sought reconciliation and forgiveness from those who have been oppressed and downtrodden. This has driven out some of the wrong negative thought patterns and attitudes between the people of our nation. This has created an initial victory of vacancy. But there must also be a positive turning away from these thought patterns by the <u>very groups who have been downtrodden and oppressed</u>. Victory with occupancy will be the swiftest and the most powerful when the effects and influences of wrong agreements and walls between people begin to be torn down by those from within the very heart of the groups who have been hurt the most.

Placing of blame will not solve the hurt ones' deepest pain and fear. Agreeing with the victimization that has taken place will never de-victimize those who have been hurt the most by it. Healing of attitudes, reaching unity in thinking, finding common grounds for understanding, and the grace and mercy of God alone will solve that and more. How can this happen? When all peoples agree upon one prayer, one plea, one common cry, one unified hope: *"Not my will, not my religious denomination's will, not my race's will, not my gender's will, not my culture's will, but THY WILL BE DONE, O LORD."* There is not really any other direction we can ever move towards in true unity.

God has said, *"Seek the peace and prosperity of the city to which I carried you into exile. Pray to God for it, because if it prospers, you too will prosper."* (Jeremiah 29:7, NIV). It is God's will for the territorial and demonic strongholds over our cities to be destroyed. How do you close an open door of access to a territorial spirit or a satanic prince over a given area? You loose reverse, and undo existing corporate wrong agreements. You occupy the territory won by praying corporate right agreement over it. You pray this way, as an individual and corporately with others:

Territorial Strongholds Prayer

Father, I (we) thank you for your Word. I (we) thank you for the wisdom and skill of understanding that you are willing to impart to me (us). Cause my (our) heart(s) to seek to receive revelation from you as purely as you desire to give it, without interjecting my (our) opinions, judgments, or self-personalization upon

240

it. You are not a God who desires to hide answers from those who are genuinely seeking them. But you will hide truth from those who believe they already have all of the answers.

Lord, my (our) city (church, family, nation, etc.) desperately needs revival. In your Word, you have said, **If my people who are called by name shall humble <u>themselves</u>, pray, seek, crave, and require of necessity my face, and turn from their wicked ways, then will I hear from heaven, forgive their sin, and heal their land . . . my eyes will be opened, and my ears attentive to prayer offered . . .** *(2 Chronicles 7:14-15, AMP). Lord, let this be so in me (us) now.*

Before I can ever be a part of a corporate prayer of right agreement, I now humble myself before you. Forgive me and forgive my people (family, church, culture, race, gender, etc.) for our sins and wrong actions towards you and others, but forgive me especially for sins of omission. Forgive me for all of the times I have not obeyed your Word and reached out to others, the times I have chosen to cling to my own comfort rather than to follow your instructions to go to the captives and set them free.

I repent of my own shallowness in praying only small prayers. Give me a revelation of the pain of those lost in darkness, and those who are in bondage. Teach me how to pray big prayers in full faith. I choose to surrender my will to your greater purposes. I choose to bind myself body, soul, and spirit to your will for my life. I will seek those who will do likewise, and together we shall come into right agreement for your will to be done on earth as you have already established it in heaven.

241

Because of the oppression, the pillaging, and the abuse of those who have suffered in our land and in other lands, there have been many wrong agreements struck in hurting, needy, angry, hating hearts. Lord, I am (we are) now concerned about the multiplied wrong agreements that have created the doors of demonic access over our immediate cities and surrounding lands. Father, I (we) loose, crush, smash, destroy, shatter, dissolve, and disrupt the controlling effects, influences, and power tactics of the territorial spirits that are feeding off the corporate pain, hatred, and fear resident within the abused and wronged now living in as well as those who have formerly lived in this area. I (we) loose these spirits' smothering clouds of anger, hatred, and fear that have caused the "groups, races, cultures, genders, social classes, etc." of the area to disengage from and distrust each other so much.

These territorial spirits have perpetuated generational bondage thinking patterns—one hating, hurting, fearful generation teaching the next generation to hate, to hurt, and to fear. I (we) loose, crush, smash, destroy, and shatter the effects, influences, and power of the multiplied corporate wrong agreements that have opened up doorways of access to invading forces of darkness over our homes and cities. I (we) bind the minds, wills, and emotions of every person in this area to the mind of Christ. Using my (our) Kingdom keys, I (we) bind every individual in this area to your will, God, and to the emotional healing of the Holy Spirit. I (we) loose these territorial spirits' control over those whose corporate wrong thoughts and attitudes have spawned strongholds justifying hate and anger, acts of retribution and distrust.

I (we) also loose the wrong attitudes and

strongholds out of the souls of every person living in this area. I (we) loose traditional thought bondage, religious thought bondage, cultural thought bondage, intellectual thought bondage, and poverty-based bondage thinking from everyone in this area. I (we) loose the wrong thoughts, attitudes, assumptions, mindsets, and strongholds from my (our) own soul(s) as well.

By abundant acts of your mercy and grace, open up avenues of pursuit for me (us) to earnestly search for right agreements in prayer with others. Lord, make me (us) your avenue(s), your imparters, your vessels, your hands of grace and mercy. Use me (us) to be your earthly vessels of love and reconciliation. Reveal my (our) own lack that I (we) might become healed and available to have "this treasure within my (our) earthly vessels," always ready to give out. Use me (us) to speak your words of healing. Show me (us) what attitudes and fears reside within my (our) own soul(s) that have prevented me (us) from doing this before now, and I (we) will loose them.

As we gaze into each others' eyes, face to face, race to race, let us always see the other person as a man, a woman, a young person, a child that Jesus Christ died for. Regardless of our former ways of thinking, let us look only upon each person we meet as one whom Jesus Christ shed His blood for. Let our vision always be that those who can be turned from their pain and sorrow and unforgiveness to wait upon (bind themselves to) the Lord—expecting, looking for, and hoping in His goodness and love—shall renew their strength and power, shall rise up closer to God, shall run and not be weary, shall walk and not faint or become tired.

Let your mighty Holy Spirit serve notice on the territorial spirits over this territory that there are people "doing" that which needs to be done to unseat them. We will not only unseat them, but we will occupy the land, and forever prevent their return. Father, don't let us just seek victory by creating a vacancy. Let us press on through and hold the territory as we all begin to agree on the only thing we could ever all agree upon to bring healing to our land: That your will be done, Father. Not our wills, never our wills; but **YOUR WILL BE DONE.** *Amen.*

10

Producing Your Promise

Revival Is Coming

Revival is coming! Big revival. Undeniable revival. Fall on your face before the power of God revival. *Revival fire!* No matter how many unsurrendered souls seek to distract the Church from it, it's coming. No matter how many fearful, doubting lambs fear it will never happen, it's coming. I feel like I'm writing an advertising "trailer" for a movie about a gigantic meteor headed for earth, but no movie could ever hope to show power like the power of God when it explodes. It's coming! Don't ask God to give you a desire to pray for revival, ask God to throw you right into the middle of revival fire's burning and birthing process.

We've all sat around praying for God to give us a desire to be a part of the preparation process of revival.

I hope sincerely hope no one misses the purpose for the preparation. I remember hearing Mary Ann Brown from Texas once tell a hilarious story about her daughter's pregnancy. As I remember the story, the daughter asked Mary Ann to be present at the birth. Mary Ann promptly reminded her daughter about how she always fainted at the sight of blood. "So, dear," she continued logically, "you can surely see that you don't want me in the delivery room. I'd be more trouble than help."

The daughter archly reminded her mother of a Scripture that all preacher mothers love to quote to their children (natural or spiritual) as she said, "Excuse me? Aren't you the one who says you can do all things through Christ who strengthens you?" (See Philippians 4:13, NKJ). Preacher mothers and preacher fathers often find those kinds of verses coming home to roost when their souls offer excuses for why they can't do something.

Mary Ann knew she was trapped. So she began to take classes to prepare for her delivery room experience. She began to read up on everything she could, and she prayed mightily for a deliverance from blood-induced fainting spells. Finally she announced, "All right, I have prepared, I have prayed, I'm ready." The day of the birth arrived and Mary Ann marched confidently into the delivery room with her daughter. It only took one loud scream accompanied by one gush of blood, and Mary Ann fainted on the spot. She woke up in the recovery room on a gurney next to her daughter after the birth was over.

Mary Ann's delivery of this story was so funny, I hurt myself laughing. But her point for telling the story was sobering and insightful. She had gone through great preparation to try to prepare for the experience of her daughter's delivery of a new grandchild. Then she passed out and missed the whole purpose for the preparation—the birth itself. Many of God's children today are trying to get themselves ready for the biggest show out that God has ever visited upon His Church. We must not get right up to the point of birthing the promise and then pass out before the birth. We don't want to wake up and find out that we missed the best part of our days here on earth!

God's people need to recognize their potential for quick birthings of God-ordained promises just like the children birthed of the Hebrew women in Exodus 1:19. The midwives said, *"The Hebrew women are not like the Egyptian women; they are vigorous and quickly delivered; their babies are born before the widwife comes to them"* (AMP). Let me reprase this verse to reflect how I see it applying to God's end times people: "God's people are not like the people of the world, they are vigorous and produce the promises of God quickly; their promises are birthed without any human help."

Christian, anything now standing between you and your destiny can be dealt with quickly and efficiently with the keys of the Kingdom. There is no need to go over a list here of what to bind and loose, for this book and the previous two books of this trilogy have more than belabored such lists. There is nothing left to do now but to begin to cooperate with the labor pains that are already quickening within you. Don't ask God to give you a desire to do it, just do it! Having birthed three children, I have to smile at the thought of a pregnant woman in labor being asked if she wants prayer for a desire to birth that baby. No, that's beyond a smile. That's a knee slapper!

If you have read this far, you are already standing at the door of the delivery room, perhaps even having assumed the birthing position. You can't go back, in fact all you can do is get out of the way of the promise coming forth. Get your assignment clear, get your understanding clear, then follow clear through.

We are predestined to fulfill God's purposes according to His will. Nothing in God's purposes has to turn upon your will. But it will be less heart stopping if He can fulfill His purposes in you without your will trying to bail out every time it thinks He's about to slow down. God's presence is revving up in your life–make room for it. Seek to be aligned with His will, turn away from anything that would distract you from this. If you have any anxiety, stress, fear, lack of direction, a sense of "the bottom falling out," your soul is in the driver's seat of your life. Drop kick it out of there. Get the magnifying glass off your own life and your problems and turn it towards heaven to magnify the Lord instead. Stop magnifying your own fear before you scare yourself to death!

God Knows All About It

God has told me many times that He knows all about every hard situation Christians have ever found themselves broken by and tangled up in. He has reassured me, *"All you need to do is get them to a position where they will take down their walls and let me get in to heal them. That's all I've called you to do. You don't have to understand every hellish thing that man or woman can get themselves into. I do, and I'm not grossed out, all right? I'll deal with all that. You just teach them how to let me inside of their defense systems. I won't blow those systems up, for that would be a violation of their souls. I do not want to violate their souls, I want my sons and daughters to voluntarily surrender and entrust their whole being to me. That is the only way we can have true intimacy, for real intimacy is always voluntary. Forced intimacy is violation. You teach them how to take down the walls that their souls have put up to keep me out. I'll do the rest."*

What a relief to know that He has not called me to be responsible for having to know so many things that I can't possibly fully understand. He's only called me to be responsible for what He has taught me to do—teach others how to use the keys of the Kingdom in prayer, binding and loosing, to deconstruct the control center of their unsurrendered souls. God has not called me to be a midwife. My function is to help get people undressed—stripped of their old ragged garments and graveclothes—and into the delivery room of the mighty Doctor of heaven for the birthing process. I'm also supposed to simultaneously help them get to the chapel for the funeral of their old man. I am to help them get past themselves so they can get where they need to go. God conducts the births and the funerals.

Headlines and Billboard Faces

Do you want to know how you're doing in these final days? Look in the mirror when you are having a hard day. Your face is a barometer of your soul's "state of mind," regardless of your attempts to project a good countenance. God sees right through it, Satan sees right through it, and most of your family and friends do, too. Your eyes (the lights of your countenance), your voice (the sound of your words, tone, volume), and your actions (the outward manifestations of your inward attitude) are all like CNN headline previews of the real story in your soul. Your face is the photo op, your words are the sound bites, and your actions are the latest breaking news report in your life. It may be the only report much of the world ever reads. Is your soul living in the same state as your born again spirit, or is your soul living in another state entirely? You can say anything you want, sound as smart as you want, act as spiritual as you want, raise your hands, and shout hallelujah. But what are your countenance, words, and actions manifesting? They are manifesting the condition of your soul within you.

Is the top story in your soul heralded by this headline? EXTRA! EXTRA! READ ALL ABOUT IT! CHRIST IS ABUNDANTLY ABLE TO FIX ALL OF THIS AS I COOPERATE WITH HIS WILL AND HIS WAYS.

Or, is the top story in your soul heralded by this headline? CHRIST CAN'T HELP ME, CHRIST DOESN'T CARE. HE PROBABLY WANTS ME HOMELESS, ALONE, AND BROKE. HE WON'T PROVIDE FOR ME. HE CAN'T SAVE MY CHILDREN. HE JUST HASN'T BEEN AND ISN'T ALL I NEED. If this is your headline/billboard, it is time for you to have a paradigm shift in your thinking. You are seeing God's promises and the truth of His Word through your skewed perceptions of it. You need to bring your perception of what God has done, is doing, and wants to do, into alignment with the reality of His immutable, unchangeable, undeniably true promise for you.

Obeying the One Who Loves Us Most

We ALL need a paradigm shift in our thinking about why God created us and what He is expecting of us. We do not need to be more powerful and more authoratative, we just need to get better at staying out of His way. We need to surrender all of our fine preparation for this hour, even if it has helped us to lay down our wills—and just simply obey. Once the promise is bursting forth out of us, further preparation is useless anyway. We need to be light on our feet with fruit bubbling up out of our spirits, ready to dance or march or just walk.

Remember that Enoch didn't build an ark, he didn't lead millions through the wilderness, he didn't write a book of the Bible, he didn't call fire down out of heaven, he didn't slay a giant, he just walked with God. And that pleased God tremendously. Can you just walk? Then there is hope for you. It doesn't matter whether we are rich or beautiful or strong or intellectual or not! Every one of us, tall or small, young or old, slender or stout, any level of intelligence, any type of personality, can just walk with God. Remember, He is only asking us to walk with Him to where He wants us to be when He needs an instrument to transmit His power and anointing through. He prefers to do all of the power stuff himself.

Soul to Spirit Transition Crisis

At one point in my Christian walk, just prior to getting the binding and loosing revelation God has given to me, everything seemed to crash in my life. I had a genuine, mid-life, spiritual identity crisis—a big one. So much seemed to spin out of my control, I fell apart.

251

My pastor suggested that I go up into the mountains and see an old friend, a mature woman of God who had been through many trials and tribulations during a lifelong walk and ministry for the Lord. I drove into her little compound on a ranch high in the mountains of Northern California, drug myself out of the car, and then began to haul several heavy suitcases towards the house. "What in the world do you have in those cases, Liberty—rocks?" my hostess asked, laughing at my struggles.

I replied that I had all of my dying-to-self, crucifying-of-the-flesh, killing-the-old-man, mortifying-my-members, books with me and I was going to die or else! I was quite serious about crucifying everything of me, perhaps even becoming a monk or a nun and withdrawing from the human struggle as the world knows it. She cocked her head wisely, and spoke a few words I will never forget, "I think you need to lighten up, my friend. Let's go for a ride and let me show you our little mountain town."

I was rather crushed that she didn't see the importance of my quest to get everything out of the way between me and God, once and for all. But I obediently followed her to the car and off we went. While riding through town, I noticed an art and print supply shop and asked her to stop so I could get something. Going inside, I found exactly what I wanted—several big colored markers and a large pad of newsprint. I told my friend I wanted to go home and try to graphically diagram the abstract feelings that were still sweeping over me.

So, back at the ranch house, I positioned myself and my colored markers, and stared at the newsprint pad. My friend offered, "Since you seem to be overwhelmed with multiple trials, why don't you list them all and see if there's any pattern." That sounded like a good idea and so I began to record the mental list that had originally plunged me into despair when I compared it to a stress test in a magazine I had picked up a week earlier. This stress test was supposed to be an early warning signal of a possible breakdown. Ten points for this, five points for that, different assigned points for different things that had happened in your life during the previous 12 months. Then you added the points and checked it against a scale to see if you needed help.

In 12 months time I had experienced 18 areas of turmoil listed as major stress points in a life: I had been through a nasty church split, I lost my pastor, I changed jobs, my new job required moving to another town, I had to sell the first home I had ever purchased on my own, I had a fire in my kitchen the night before I moved out, I had major surgery, I had a teenager run away, I had major financial distress, I had family relationship problems, and on and on. I was completely off the end of the danger list of this stress warning guide, probably in an unlisted category that should have been called: Surely Already Dead.

As I sat staring at the list with great doom and gloom circling me, I decided this had not been such a good idea after all. Right there before me was a record of why I was about to implode because of stress. My friend stepped up, looked over my shoulder, and said, "You have already moved, right? You have worked your way into the new job, right? Your teenager came home, right? Why don't you put a check mark beside each item that is no longer open ended and unfinished?"

So, I began to go down the list. I'm in a nice new church, check. I have another pastor I like, check. I sold my home, check. My teenager came home, check. My finances are better, check. My surgery is healed, check." Suddenly I realized that out of the eighteen items on the list, only three were still awaiting resolution. I jumped up and shouted, "Look at this! This is graphic, recorded, technicolor proof that I am not a loser or a victim. I can overcome—even in the middle of a hurricane of circumstances. I can do all things through Christ, He has made me an overcomer. Hallelujah!!!" And I began to dance around the room.

What I needed was someone and something to jog me into a paradigm shift in my thinking. I had been through so much, I did not realize that I had settled into a mindset of seeing disaster everywhere I looked. I was looking at life through sad, hurting eyes that had become so weighted down, they no longer looked up at God to see the promise He saw in me. I recognized that I was turned around and upside down, which obviously makes it difficult to know which way is forward and onward. We all just need to shift our perspective and see what God sees for our futures and to quit going over and over the old things that aren't going to help us get there! One woman said to me after a meeting, "I hear what you're saying, and I feel like I've been trying to wash my clothes in the dryer. No wonder things haven't been working the way they should!"

Too many people say, "I know I'll never be perfect until I get to heaven." Perhaps not perfect, but you can be in the center of His will and allowing Him to work it perfectly through your life every day. Take another look at the phrase "being perfect," and apply it to Christ's

Seed of life within you instead of your own efforts at life. You're not, but it is. Remember I said earlier that our destiny is just to be holy dirt for that Seed? How holy does dirt have to be to be just the soil for a life-filled Seed to grow in?

Not About You Anymore

Today our churches are filled with people more interested in experiences than in growth and change. Pastors struggling to disciple their congregations often end up preaching to peoples' needs rather than pushing them towards their destinies. People in the pews have been focusing on: "How does this affect me?" This is focusing on a wrong agreement that the preaching is meant to make them feel better. Lord, focus your people on the right agreement that good preaching pushes and pressures them to let your promise loose.

We never will be able to relax in perfect security in His love until we are absolutely convinced, totally believing, and willing to abide in the knowledge that Christ's Seed of life is growing and anxious to bear fruit through our lives every minute. This requires a relaxing and a resting in Him, a knowing that He has everything under control regardless of difficult moments. As soon as we get uptight our souls get involved again, and we hinder the flow of His life, His love, and His power coming through us.

We can't deal in our own strength with the unbelievable cross section of mankind that life will present us with—angry people, abusive people, cross people, devious people—acquaintances, strangers, difficult family members. We must move towards humanity in the flow of His love, or we may cause more problems than we will bring solutions. It is so much easier to move in His flow when you've taken the reins away from your soul's control. This brings a freedom somewhat like removing a heavy yoke and harness from a horse and then seeing Dobbin head out into the pasture to roll in the grass and kick box the air!

"God is love. When we take up permanent residence in a life of love, we live in God and God lives in us. This way, love has the run of the house, becomes at home and mature in us, so that we're free of worry on Judgment Day—our standing in the world is identical with Christ's. There is no room in love for fear. Well-formed love banishes fear. Since fear is crippling, a fearful life—fear of death, fear of judgment—is one not yet fully formed in love. We, though, are going to love—love and be loved. First we were loved, now we love. He loved us first. If anyone boasts, 'I love God,' and goes right on hating his brother or sister, thinking nothing of it, he is a liar. If he won't love the person he can see, how can he love the God he can't see? The command we have from Christ is blunt: Loving God includes loving people. You've got to love both" (1 John 4:16-21, *The Message*).

Know the Truth and It Will Set You Free

Jesus walked right into the center of the entrenched religion of His day and proclaimed a new view of holiness. This view declared that men are neither cleansed nor defiled by any outward form of behavior, rather they would henceforth be cleansed or defiled by the inward thoughts of their hearts. This was truth, but the truth alone will not set anyone free. There are many people in bondage to and living under a continual dark cloud of hard consequences in their lives while the Bible sits on their coffee table. Near proximity to truth doesn't work, for truth is not absorbed into the Christian's inner being by osmosis. Truth is not established in the Christian's inner being by getting up in the morning and verbally stating that you are putting on the armor of God. Truth must be tried, tested, used, worked out, and experienced in its fullness to *know* it. *"To the Jews who had believed him, Jesus said, 'If you hold to my teaching, you are really my disciples. Then you will* know *the truth, and the truth will set you free'"* (John 8:31-32, NIV). There must be an intimate interaction with truth to *know* it, which is far beyond just being exposed to it.

We must set our wills towards the goal of becoming the truth of who God says we are: new creatures, blessed, end times messengers, overcomers, warriors of the faith. No longer tie-a-knot-in-the-end-of-your-rope and hang on, baby Christians—but full grown, chain breaking, prison door smashing, warriors of the faith! We have enormous reason to hope, to reach, to stretch, to grow, and to expect to be fully and faithfully used of God.

Faith's Complete Commitment

Faith requires 100 percent commitment to the ground-level belief that God is good. Once again, many of the Greek words translated as faith in the original manuscripts of the New Testament mean "trust and confidence in God." This means you commit all of your concerns to Him, trusting and being confident that He knows how to resolve everything for the best. Imagine that you were struggling with flying to another country, hesitant and perhaps a little fearful, yet certain God had told you to go. You finally decided to go, but to be on the "safe side" you only commited 90 percent of yourself to get on the plane. You wanted to hold back just 10 percent of yourself in case something went wrong on the flight. When you commit to flying somewhere, all of you has to get on the plane. You can't leave your head, your hand, or your feet behind. All of you has to go or none of you goes. God didn't ask Jesus to just die a little, or cut off an arm or a leg to shed His blood. Jesus' death on the Cross was a total and complete commitment to the Father's will. So was His resurrection, hallelujah! God didn't just resurrect an arm or a leg at a time either, He brought Him up and out of the grave gloriously together and ready for His eternal destiny!

A real commitment of your faith, your trust and confidence in the goodness of God, means no back door to bail out of, no partial holding back in case God doesn't get it worked out right, no holding onto your personal agendas and plans. This is not to force you into a martyr's sense of having to commit to a potential firing squad. This is to get you to stop dragging every contingency you can think of into every situation you might face.

Evans' *Daily With The King* devotional (Moody Press) puts this so well, "The baggage laden disciple is simply asking to be swept out of the race . . . .The Lord says, 'Strip yourself for battle,' and I load myself with every thingamajig in the armory because I have to be prepared for every eventuality . . . . Lord, help me to say yes to Your defintion of what is basic and no to my continual sin of clutter."

He Loves You, Believe It!

First John 4:18, *"There is no fear in love; but perfect love casts out fear, because fear involves punishment, and the one who fears is not perfected in love"* (NAS). Adam Clarke (in his commentary writings) says with regard to 1 John 4:18 containing the phrase (He that feareth), that the Christian who has fear in his heart is still uncertain concerning his interest in Christ. (He) has not yet received the abiding witness of the Spirit that he is begotten of God; or has not yet received that fullness of love to God and man which excludes the enmity of the carnal mind.

I have often heard faith described as being like a physical muscle, a very good analogy. A physical muscle must be exercised and stretched to grow, or it will atrophy and shrivel from lack of use. You are not in a spiritual exercise program every Sunday morning at church, you are in a spiritual dining room eating spiritual food. Spiritual exercise of the faith muscle only occurs when you are confronted with something that requires you to act beyond your own ability. You cannot know whether or not you have faith to move mountains without actually interacting with some mountains (natural or spiritual). It helps to be practicing your faith on some ant hills and some small foothills all the time, rather than just waiting for a mountain to show up in your living room.

Mountains have a propensity for showing up in the most unexpected and unwelcome times of pressure and pain. When they do, the mountain must not be viewed as a potential disaster—instead, it must be recognized as another opportunity to trust that your God is able, no matter how big the mountain.

Why is trust such a factor with faith? We are unable to fathom the depths of this Almighty Lord of ours, so in lieu of understanding what He is doing at any given time, we can only trust that whatever He will do will be best. We have to understand that it certainly will be better than anything we come up with. We do not understand how He will ever do many things most of the time, so we simply must trust that He will. Faith says, "I don't know what this means, but I trust God anyhow." Trust means, "I will obey whatever you say, God, even if I don't get what I think I want." Anyone can trust and obey an authority figure if they are are convinced they will get their own way in the end. That is not trust and obedience to Christ.

It must become immaterial to us whether or not we get healed, get money, or get whatever else we want. We must simply obey what He tells us to do. After we obey, everything else is God's business. We must be willing to let God be unreasonable, according to our logic and reasoning. Only the unbeliever is foolish enough to demand that a just God justify what He does.

Acting on Faith Pleases Him

Hebrews 11:6 tells us, *"Without faith it is impossible to please him, for he that cometh to God must believe that he is, and that he is a rewarder of them that diligently seek Him."* The original Greek word translated as faith in this verse *(pistis)* means conviction that God exists and is the creator and ruler of all things. If you are not fully convinced that God exists and is the creator and ruler of all things, you cannot please Him no matter what you do! Thayer's Greek/English Lexicon says that holiness is fidelity in observing our obligations to Him. So, bringing holiness down out of an ethereal, celestial realm of meaning, we could say this instead: One who is holy feels completely obligated to do His will to please Him.

James 2:22, 24, 26 (NIV), *"His (Abraham) faith and his actions were working together, and his faith was made complete by what he did . . . . You see that a person is justified by what he does and not by faith alone . . . . As the body without the spirit is dead, so faith without deeds is dead."* Simply to read the Word and say we believe it is not enough. We must take some form of action as if we believe it will be done. We must do something to solidify our abstract faith regarding that which we say we believe. A close friend once said to me that she believed she might have an anointing for healing in her hands. I asked her what she was doing about it and she replied that she was waiting for God to give her an opportunity to use it.

I try very hard to always balance truth with grace, but sometimes familiarity with a long-time acquaintance or family member makes that hard! I rather sternly confronted this seventy-year old saint who has been a Christian since early childhood. Considering the hundreds, perhaps even thousands of people in hospitals, rest homes, hospices, in our city who would be so grateful for someone to come and minister to them, I stared at her. "Opportunity? Opportunity?" I barked. "Are you serious? There are opportunities every where you turn. What are you waiting for?"

Rather startled, she replied, "I guess I'm just afraid that I will disappoint God."

Believing I heard God speak otherwise, I spoke even more directly, "You're not afraid of disappointing

God, you're afraid of being criticized by others for believing that God would use you to do such a thing. You need to loose 'fear of people' out of your soul."

She replied that she had been loosing "fear of people," but nothing seemed to be happening. This was not the first time I have had people tell me that they have loosed and loosed something and felt nothing happened. God shot a revelation past my soul and impressed me to say, "You need to step right into the middle of this area where you have been loosing old patterns of thinking that always result in you fearing what others will say. You need to occupy that area with an action, you need to step where you have feared to go because someone might think you weren't good enough or spiritual enough. Your faith in the keys of loosing is worthless without an action on your part that agrees that your fear of man has been loosed and is gone!"

With tears and a glimmer of hope in her eyes, she said, "What do I need to do, what kind of an act?"

I said, "How about you get up this next Saturday morning, pray, and drive to a rest home. Walk in and request permission to talk to the people and pray for them. Then head for the nearest door, walk into that room, and start talking to whoever is there. Don't try to pick and choose whoever looks easiest to approach, just go up to the first people you see and ask if they would like a little company for awhile. Let them talk for a few minutes until you know what their main concerns and fears are. Then ask if you can pray with them about those concerns and fears. Prove to yourself that your prayers of loosing fear of people have worked."

She did exactly that! Shortly thereafter, she had another woman going with her to this rest home every Saturday. She even turned down a chance to go out to dinner with me and another friend on a Friday night because she wanted to write something personal in Valentine cards to take to the people in the rest home on one Saturday. After a few weeks, she came and asked me what I thought about her teaching a Bible study on *Shattering Your Strongholds* in an apartment building near her church. She began to understand about taking her faith that God wanted to use her and applying it to an action, a deed, a good work that proved she was in agreement body, soul, and spirit with what she declared that she believed. She's moving right into her destiny ministry, working hand in hand with God. Seventy is a great age to begin an end-times messenger ministry!

In Psalm 103:1, we are told that our soul should bless the Lord with all that is within us; our soul should bless His holy name. Psalm 103:5 (AMP) says He *"satisfies your mouth, your necessity and desire at your personal age, with good; so that your youth, renewed, is like the eagle's (strong, overcoming, soaring)!"*

God Doesn't Care What Others Expect of You

We need to loose the hold our souls have of other people's expectations of us, beliefs about us, and plans for us. They are not the same as God's! We also need to quit reacting to other people's stronghold thinking about us. Our wrong reactions to others' strongholds can send us over the waterfalls in a barrel, and then we have to repent and release wrong thoughts about the people (not so easy in a barrel!). Or, worst of all, we may try to hang onto our wrong thoughts and work at justifying and rationalizing doing so. Justification and rationalizing your reactions to other peoples' reactions is just like cross-pollination—strongholds spawning strongholds.

We should be too busy gleefully tearing down our own stronghold thinking to worry about reacting to theirs. Gleeful because we realize that maybe just one more has to come down and that rush of the river of life will begin to pour through our riverbed. When we finally break through into contentment at all times as Paul had in the following verse, we will no longer react to people or to our circumstances. Think of the extra time and energy we will recoup! Paul told the Philippians, *"I have learned to be content whatever the circumstances. I know what it is to be in need, and I know what it is to have plenty. I have learned the secret of being content in any and every situation, whether well fed or hungry, whether living in plenty or in want. I can do everything through him who gives me strength"* (Philippians 4:11-13, NIV).

Help Me, God

I heard a story that made the natural consequences of reacting very real to me. A Christian teen I'll call Bobby, a high school sophomore on the varsity basketball team, had been having a really, really bad week. He had almost come to the conclusion that God didn't even care about him, let alone love him. Things just kept getting worse and worse, sending his attitude and his reactions into a further spiraling downward. Bobby's father said to him one morning, "Son, next time you get in a tough spot, don't get mad. God loves you and wants to help you. Just ask Him, because He really does care."

That day evolved into another bad day, with Bobby struggling to keep on track with his class schedule. After his sixth period class, Bobby knew he had to rush to his locker and get his sports gear, then sprint to the the team bus that would take the team members to basketball practice. If anybody missed this particular team bus to the practice, they were off the team. After a really hard week, Bobby had concluded that God wasn't really paying much attention to anything in his life, so it was all up to him. He ran out of his final class and down the hall, skidded to a stop in front of his locker, tried to open it, and the locker jammed.

Completely frustrated and at the end of his rope, he began to bang on his locker, angrily saying, "God, you really don't care, do you? You just don't care about what happens to me, you don't care about anything that's important to me, you don't . . . ."

Then he suddenly remembered what his father had said to him that morning. "Son, the next time you are in trouble, don't lose your temper and get mad. Just ask God to help you." Bobby was standing in front of a jammed locker which was a natural fact. The team bus was loading and about to leave—a natural fact. But as his father's words went through his head once more, this young man stepped off the unfriendly court of the natural facts he was facing and over onto the supernatural home court advantage where God's team gathered. He said, "God, I am sorry. Help me."

Right then, a janitor came around the corner wearing his tool belt, heard Bobby's plea for help and quickly removed a specific tool and unjammed the locker. Bobby grabbed his gear, ran out the door, and made it onto the bus. Had Bobby just stood there and beat on his jammed locker, <u>trapped by the wrong belief</u> <u>that the natural facts were all there was to his life,</u> he would have had to walk out the consequences of his belief in those facts (bye bye, basketball team). But he stepped out of their natural grip and said, "God, help me." God's supernatural truth can change a natural fact in a second.

Saint Stoner to Apostle

As Paul grew in Christ, he felt His love so strongly that nothing moved him. Paul said he was not moved by whatever might be ahead of him—even to the point of not counting his life dear. His only goal was to finish his race and fulfill his allotted earthly destiny for Christ with joy. Wow! What an incredible example he has set for us. The remarkable thing is that this is truly attainable by each one of us. The goal of these three books has been to show you that the Seed of life He has planted within you knows exactly how to fulfill the individual race and ministry that has been ordained for you and even now is already completely mapped out in heaven.

Are ready to step into this destiny? It certainly won't do you any good to ask yourself if you are ready. Asking your own soul something like that is like asking a compulsive liar if he is telling you the truth. You have no way of knowing whether or not you are getting a straight answer. There is really only one way you can truly tell if you are getting an honest answer about your spiritual growth: God allows you to go through something that has always caused you to fall apart— and then the day comes when you go through it again and it doesn't faze you. This time you go right on through, out the other side, refined like gold, without even the smell of smoke on you. You know you are ready to see God start setting some destiny dates. And God is ready to begin to bring forth His supplies for your assignment.

Hudson Taylor said, "God's work done in God's ways will never lack God's supplies." Never try to do God's will according to your will or you're liable to lack a lot! We must stop looking at what we don't have and what we might even lose if we obey God without any regard for our own personal needs. We must seek the Kingdom of God first, and realize that all other things we need will be added to us. We are not being called to give away everything that has ever meant anything to us—but we will be called to give up that which is so important to us that it can cause us to pull back from abandoning all to Him. God really just wants one thing—that we surrender and obey. We don't have to figure out how to save the world, we just need to get rid of our reasoning that says we just can't be who He created us to be. We can do this. We can give up our agendas and let Him work out His agenda through us. We can give up our plans and let Him work out His plans through us. We can pray:

I want what you want, God, even if they never say that they're sorry, even if they never say that they were wrong. I want what you want, even if they never say I was right, even if they never say that I deserve to be repaid. I want what you want, God, more than I want to get even, more than I want to be recognized for what I've done, more than I want to be appreciated for what I went through. I want what you want, God, more than I want that wrong relationship, more than I want fulfilled fantasies, more than I want control, more than

I want others held accountable for what they did. I want what you want, God, more than I want my own way. No matter what it costs my soul, I want what you want, God!

Will I Get All My Desires Fulfilled?

Some of us will be called to submit our lives totally unto Christ alone for the short time left on this earth. Others will walk out their earthly destinies with a human mate. When you are truly surrendered to the Lord, having stripped away your self-defense mechanisms over your deepest unmet needs, unhealed hurts, and unresolved issues to receive His healing, you really won't care which path He chooses for you. You will be fully content in whatever state He wants you in—single or married. The key phrase here is *whatever state He wants you in*. If this statement strikes any twinge or chord of fear, disappointment, or discouragement in your soul, that is all right. It has only served a purpose to alert you that you still have unmet needs and desires buried in your soul. You have the keys of the Kingdom to open them up to God for healing if you choose. Just don't let them cause you to hold back from receiving all of His divine destiny plans and purposes for you in these last days on earth.

It is your soul that cannot conceive that Jesus Christ could be enough right now. It is the soul that worries the previous statement might mean that those now unmarried will not have a spouse, a family, a home filled with children in the time remaining here on earth. If He has not yet been allowed deep enough within you to show you that He is more than able to fulfill your every desire, let Him into the deepest recesses of your soul to reveal to you the plans He has for your future. He is able to exceed and excel the most charming of princes, the most beautiful of princesses, the most adorable of children.

For about the first 15 years of my Christian walk, I had a fear (diminishing ever so slightly as each year passed by) that if I let God know I was satisfied at any level below what I felt I needed be happy, He would say, "She's fine, leave her there." Consequently, I never really relaxed and fully enjoyed so many of the blessings He gave to me every day. I was always a little bit afraid that if I did, God would think I was willing to settle for less than I actually needed.

Jesus Christ is not only more than enough right now, His love is a treasure to be coveted and sought. He is worth pursuing and eager to be caught. He is richer, more attractive, more congenial, more exciting, more loyal, more faithful, more loving, funnier, warmer, dearer, kinder, than any human being who ever lived. He has waited a long time for you to realize just how close He is to you. He is waiting right there inside of your spirit, waiting to burst forth through your soul and your body. Waiting to burst forth into your life. Lay down all of your expectations of what you think you want from this temporal life. Your finite expectations are so far below what He wants to give to you as His eternal bride. He is the perfect Promise.